sweet enough

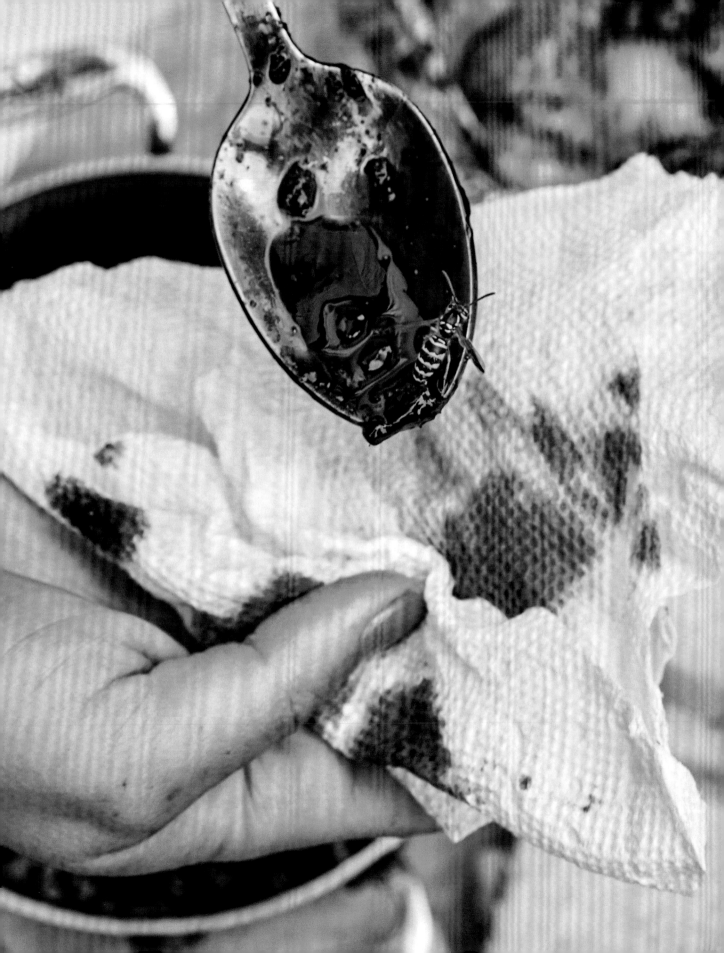

sweet enough

alison roman

Clarkson Potter / Publishers
New York

photographs by
chris bernabeo

is not made
to be a crumb.
—
Mary Oliver

Published in the United States
by Clarkson Potter/Publishers,
an imprint of Random House,
a division of Penguin Random
House LLC, New York.
clarksonpotter.com

CLARKSON POTTER is a
trademark and POTTER with
colophon is a registered
trademark of Penguin Random
House LLC.

Library of Congress Cataloging-
in-Publication Data available at
lccn.loc.gov/2022029048.
LC ebook record available at
lccn.loc.gov/2022029049.

ISBN 978-1-984-82639-8
Ebook ISBN 978-1-984-82640-4

Printed in China

Photographer: Chris Bernabeo
Production Assistant: Jane Morgan
Editor: Francis Lam
Editorial Assistant: Darian Keels
Designer: Britt Cobb
Production Editor: Mark McCauslin
Production Manager: Kim Tyner
Compositors: Merri Ann Morrell
and Zoe Tokushige
Copy Editor: Kate Slate
Indexer: Elizabeth T. Parson
Marketer: Allison Renzulli
Publicist: Jana Branson

10 9 8 7 6 5 4 3 2 1

First Edition

frozen things

i've got all this fruit, now what?

morning times, snack times

staples and extras

introduction

Something I hear all the time when I bring up desserts is, "I can cook, but I can't bake." Of course, I know why people say or think that: Conventional wisdom suggests that cooking is wild and free, encouraging creativity and improvisation. Desserts, on the other hand, should be tidy and precise. Prim, proper, controlled. Scientific, even. But as someone who would never be described as tidy or precise, who is not prim or proper, who is not a scientist, I reject those sentiments.

I am, however, a person who finds joy in licking the leftover pudding at the bottom of the pot, who can't help but slice a pie before it's properly cooled just to taste the insides (even though I will tell you not to), who will buy all the short-lived sour cherries I can and frantically cook them down with an unmeasured amount of sugar so I can still taste them all year long. I am a person who wipes floury hands on their pants, who will use only one bowl to mix a cake batter if it means I don't have to wash another thing, who will avoid using anything that gets plugged in at all costs, even if (or especially when) it means whipping cream by hand. Desserts, baking, whatever we want to call it here (this book contains both desserts that are not baked and baked goods that are not dessert) should be for anyone, at any time, requiring little more than two hands and a modicum of patience.

Sweet things, by nature, are a little frivolous, which is probably why I love them. Gestures that demonstrate joy can exist just to exist, a simple but valuable reminder that desire is as important as hunger, wants as important as needs. And the gestures can be small but nevertheless significant—ripe berries sweetened with sugar and crushed into sour cream; a giant, buttery cookie topped with rainbow sprinkles. They are an additive; our lives do not depend on these mini-pleasures. We will not wither away if there is no pudding for dessert. But what a nice thing to do to remind ourselves and each other that we live for more than necessity. That there is more than practicality; there are flowers for yourself just because, a fluffy cake with candles for making it through another turn around the sun, a bowl of ripe fruit dressed with bittersweet amaro at the end of a meal because you don't want the night to end, a small sliver of cold carrot cake for breakfast because it just tastes so nice.

Generally speaking, my recipe style and aesthetic could be described as "rustic," "carefree," "approachable." My desserts tend to follow suit, a little wild-looking and decidedly unkempt. Perfect they are not; I admit that I didn't so much choose this aesthetic as this aesthetic chose me.

Rusticness aside, these recipes are intentionally simple and especially flexible. Some of the recipes don't require an oven or even a stovetop. I wanted to write a dessert book that celebrated the excellence of basicness rather than distract with needless complexities. Most have suggestions for you to fancy things up as you wish, which will always be easy when you have a great, reliable, and foolproof base recipe to start with. You have to walk before you run, etc.

My hope for you, reading this book and hopefully baking (or assembling) your way through it, is that you strive for the animalistically irresistible, not aesthetically pristine—I find the two are rarely the same. Think of the best piece of fruit you've ever had, likely falling apart on the way to your mouth, juices dribbling down your forearm. Or maybe a lasagna, too cheesy and delicious to be willingly cut into perfect squares.

Maybe I'm just compensating for the fact that despite my formal training as a pastry chef in a restaurant kitchen, combined with additional years of baking and whisking and pouring and scraping and stacking and rolling and folding, I'm still not an expert. My pies still leak, cheesecakes crack, and pound cakes are pulled from the oven before they're fully baked. Lopsided and wonky, occasionally almost burned, unevenly frosted, my desserts are consistently imperfect. But perfection is boring, and these recipes—baked longer than you think, so the edges caramelize and stay crunchy; seasoned with enough salt to taste the butter; just sweet enough with sugar to qualify as dessert, but not so much that you can't taste the sour, the bitter, the salt, and the fruit—well, damn, if they aren't delicious. And when they come out of your kitchen, I hope you, too, feel that they're full of joy, imperfections and all.

read a recipe
start to finish
before making it

There are plenty of instant gratification recipes here, and some that need a bit of planning. But regardless, please, I beg of you: Always read a recipe start to finish before you start. You will have a better understanding of what happens when, what ingredients go where, and how long you should plan to be indisposed with sweet treat making. There's nothing worse than thinking you could have cookies in 20 minutes, only to discover the dough needs to chill for two full hours before you can bake.

 Recipes that look short may belie a long chill or rest, and occasionally, one that spans two pages is just me talking too much but is actually very easy to execute. You won't know until you read it.

flour: how much does it weigh?

Great question. When I get a cup of flour from the bag using the scoop-and-level technique (scoop the flour from the bag, then use a knife to level the top—rather than spooning it into the measuring cup) and weigh it, I get between 140 and 145 grams—this is the case for nearly all one hundred people I polled (I would have done more, but who has the time). Several popular websites and brands list other amounts—some as low as 120 grams, some over 150 grams. I'm not here to say they are wrong and I am right; I'm just saying that for this specific book, all the gram conversions are based on the assumption that 1 cup of flour weighs between 140 and 145 grams. So if you have a scale, it's all good—just use the gram weight. But if you don't have a scale, be sure to use the scoop-and-level method of measuring.

Why isn't this standardized? I simply don't know. I have at least one gray hair and I think it's because of this. Maybe once I find out why a non-deep-dish Pyrex pie plate is so hard to find, or why most loaf pans are 9 × 5 inches as opposed to the more elegant, shapely 9 × 4 inches, I'll never know. The baking industrial complex is a mystery. Anyway, those grams add up and, if miscalculated, can mean a wet cake batter or an overly dry cookie dough. Yet another reason to get a scale.

but sugar always weighs the same, right?

Similarly, although perhaps less dramatically, the internet suggests one cup of sugar weighs 200 grams, which has simply never happened to me (or to my recipe testers, friends, or editor!). By my measurements and weighing, 1 cup of sugar weighs about 220g, and I'm guessing, unlike flour, it's less about how you measure and more about the brand. For those keeping track, I use Domino and my cup of sugar weighs 220g.

see also: a scale. do I need one?

Yes. I don't like to say you need to spend money on something you'll never use—but if you're considering using this book more than once (and I hope you are), I'd love it if you had a scale. Weight measurements leave little room for error: 100 grams weighs 100 grams no matter where you are or what you're weighing. But somebody's 1 cup can be different than someone else's 1 cup (see: flour)—a solid number takes the guesswork out of a lot. (Incidentally, I like to weigh in grams rather than pounds or ounces because 100 grams is a lot easier to deal with math-wise than 3.5714 ounces.)

All that said, the recipes in this book are still perfectly makeable if you don't have a scale and/or prefer to use measuring cups and spoons.

a word on ovens

If a recipe doesn't work out, I'm willing to bet it's either because of a mismeasurement of ingredients (flour, probably) or the oven. Regarding the latter: Ovens are finicky, and they're all VERY different. It's too hot, it's not hot enough, it is hot in the back but not in the front, it heats from the bottom and not from the top, you thought it should be convection but it was on roast, you thought it was on bake, but it was on convection. Ovens are a MESS.

But we are doing the best we can with what technology we have. For what cold comfort it offers, I have only ever tested recipes for my books in an oven that I would describe as "moderately functional." Small, average-in-every-way apartment ovens with effectively one setting: on or off. Hot or less hot. But there are two things I do to help assert dominance over the chaos inside our ovens:

I keep a thermometer (purchased at my local hardware store!) inside my oven to give me a better sense of what the temperature actually is, as opposed to what it's telling me it might be.

I always make sure there is an oven rack positioned in the center. Regardless if the heat source is at the bottom or the top, making sure you're baking things in the center of the oven is your first line of defense against something that burns/browns too quickly on top or bottom. If you're baking something that requires two racks (i.e., three cake pans), be sure to rotate the pans halfway through baking to give them all an even bake.

ingredients

The nice thing about baking is that most of the ingredients are pantry staples or things easily procured at even the smallest of corner stores. I deeply believe you can create great baked goods no matter the quality of ingredients or where they're purchased. That said, read on for some specifics that will assist your shopping, should you want more guidance.

Salt: If you are the type of person who always feels the need to increase the salt in the dessert recipes they use, well, I see you. I am you. But please trust that you will not have to do that here. In fact, I like salt so much that if you're not used to, ahem, appropriately seasoned desserts, you may taste these recipes and interpret some things as "salty," which I take as a compliment.

The salt in all of these recipes is kosher. I am perennially brand-agnostic about ingredients, except for my **kosher salt**. It's gotta be Diamond Crystal kosher salt, always and forever. I use it to season steak and also my cake batter. Please remember, if you are measuring with spoons, it's not a 1:1 swap for table salt or fine sea salt, which I do not advocate using here. Even other brands of kosher salt have different densities/crystal sizes, which can greatly under- or oversalt your baked goods, so buyer beware. (If you truly cannot get Diamond Crystal and only have Morton kosher salt, reduce the salt quantity in the recipe by about one-third. If you only have fine sea salt, reduce it by half. If you are measuring by weight though, just use the same weight.)

Flaky salt is a large crystal salt, flaky and delicate in texture, used as a finishing salt. This could mean during prebake, as in several of the cookie recipes, or for sprinkling on top, as with some of the tarts.

Flour: All-purpose flour unless otherwise specified. I don't ever call for self-rising because I don't trust it to be the same experience for everyone depending on the brand. When I measure my flour, I scoop the cup into the bag and level it off. My "scooped and leveled" cup weighs somewhere between 140 and 145 grams, plus or minus.

Butter: Unsalted, unless otherwise specified. I've tested and baked with the widest range of qualities, from luxe European-style to big box grocer private label. Both types work. I'm of the mind that a good recipe should taste great no matter where you got your butter or how much it costs. I also believe that if you decide that splurging for a butter with gorgeously high fat content that costs more than a whole chicken, then your baked goods will taste especially great. Choose your own adventure, but generally speaking, if I'm going to spend the money on high-quality butter, it's to serve alongside (cornbread or scones, perhaps) or use for something where the butter is undeniably front and center (shortbread, of course).

I have not exhaustively tested with nondairy butter substitutes, but I know that there are many brands out there that claim to work beautifully as a substitute without having to modify the recipe. Consult your local dairy-free baker for more specifics, though, because I have not done my homework on this matter and don't want to lead you down a bad path of faulty recommendations!

Sugar is **granulated sugar**, unless otherwise specified.

Demerara sugar is a coarse, crystalline, "partially refined" aka "raw" sugar with a pale golden brown color. Almost exclusively called for on the exterior of baked goods (cakes, cookies, pies), it adds crunchy texture and a deep caramel flavor. I also love it in my espresso. If you have difficulty locating demerara, **turbinado sugar**—widely available from Sugar in the Raw—will work in its place, although with slightly less shine. It really does make a difference, so seek it out, even if that means grabbing a few free packets next time you go to your coffee shop.

When using **light brown sugar**, **dark brown** will work in its place, and when it comes to how firmly you pack it, I don't believe in firmly packed or lightly packed light brown sugar, only "packed," which I imagine to be somewhere between lightly and firmly. Simply regularly packed is just fine by me.

As for **powdered sugar**, most organic brands will not behave the same way as good ol' commodity brands, especially in things like icing (page 184)—I don't know why, they just won't.

Eggs: The recipes in this book call for "large" eggs. Not "medium" and not "extra-large" and definitely not "jumbo." While again, any egg will work in these recipes, I will always advocate for "the good eggs." There really is a correlation between the quality of egg and the flavor/color of the yolk, which will only mean great things for your yellow cakes, various puddings, and other places where the value of an egg is truly appreciated. Fun fact: When calculating the gram conversion, the average large egg weighs approximately 50g (the white is 30g, the yolk is 20g).

Other dairy: The milk I use is **full-fat cow's milk**. Can you use alternative milks in its place? Sometimes. I can't say for certain how a recipe will behave when an oat, almond, soy, or coconut milk is used in its stead (except when I have tested, and then I mention the appropriate swaps).

Cream is **heavy cream** or **whipping cream** or "**heavy whipping cream**." For the recipes here, they are more or less interchangeable.

Buttermilk in the traditional sense is a by-product of making butter. When cream is churned, the fat solidifies into the butter, and what's left over is the buttermilk. These days, commercially available buttermilk is mostly cultured low-fat milk to mimic the real deal, clocking in somewhere between 1%–2% milkfat and labeled either "reduced fat" or "low-fat," which should be implied given the product (it would be like labeling water "wet," as our copy editor pointed out). This can be confusing to a consumer, which implies you can easily find "full-fat" buttermilk. You can't! I really wish they'd remove the "low-fat" label. I love buttermilk and always have it in my fridge, which makes sense—you'll see it used a lot in this book. Pro tip that perhaps I can't legally give: It stays good in your fridge way past the "sell-by" date. Like, weeks beyond (until it starts to smell bad or develop colorful mold).

tools

I am a technology minimalist at heart, a true luddite, and I don't believe you need much in the way of equipment to produce an excellent dessert. While a food processor and stand mixer are valuable tools to invest in, you definitely don't need either to have a great time with this book. Some of the best recipes require almost nothing at all, save for maybe a bowl, perhaps a sheet pan, and a flimsy piece of parchment. But, in a perfect world, you have a few additional pieces of "equipment" to make your experience more stress-free.

Baking sheets/sheet pan: I like regular aluminum or stainless-steel baking sheets and sheet pans, and I tend to buy mine from restaurant-supply stores (in my experience, they tend to last longer and be more affordable than what you can find marketed for the home cook). I don't care for the nonstick ones; they aren't great for roasting on, and since all baked goods should be lined with parchment anyway, why do the sheets themselves need to be nonstick? They don't. I own four regular baking sheets and am glad I do, but if that feels excessive, I recommend every household have at least two. If not for desserts, then for the chicken, for crying out loud.

Spatula: A flexible spatula. I like the ones that are silicone, which is both heat-resistant and dishwasher safe. My favorite type is the one that's one continuous piece rather than a wooden handle and removable head (stuff gets stuck in the joint and you can't wash the wood—it's just not my preference!).

Whisk: One standard, narrow whisk (not a "balloon whisk") is all you need. Small ones are cute and useful for whisking eggs or very small amounts of cream, but not a necessity.

Mixing bowls: If you don't already have a good set of mixing bowls for cooking, now's your chance to introduce a good set to your kitchen arsenal. Glass, metal, melamine—whatever you choose, it's nice to have three designated mixing bowls: small, medium, and large. Most come nested in sets of three or more, so that's good news. Worth the purchase as you'll use them for sweet, savory, and everything in between.

Pie plate: A classic 9-inch pie plate. Not deep dish. Glass is preferable to metal, as I find the heat is conducted more evenly—and being able to see the crust as it bakes is a huge assist.

Tart pan: Probably my most-used baking vessel. These typically have fluted edges and come in a variety of sizes—they are shallower than pie plates or cake pans and come with removable bottoms, which is the real reason to purchase one. I use them for chilled custard tarts, baked fruit tarts, quiche-like things, and galettes that I want to be somewhere between regular and deep-dish. I only own one, and it's a nonstick 9-inch.

Springform pan: Taller than tart pans, cake pans, and pie plates, springform pans are valued by me for their above-average height as much as their removable bottom and easy-to-remove sides. I use them to bake, chill, and freeze; for deep-dish galettes, ice cream cakes, cheesecake, icebox cakes, you name it. Any size and style springform will get use, but if you're going to purchase just one, make it a nonstick 9-inch.

Loaf pan: If you don't have a loaf pan you won't be at a total loss for things to make in this book, but you won't be able to make any of the loaf cakes. If you have no intention of making one anyway, you can skip, but it's still making the cut for me. Beyond loaf cakes, I also find them useful to freeze things like granitas, frozen yogurt, etc., and also use them to hold the demerara sugar for rolling logs of cookie dough. Loaf pans range from 9 × 5 inches to 8 × 4 inches, which makes shopping for one annoying—but regardless, the best ones (for me, anyway) always say "one pound loaf pan," are nonstick, and have straight edges.

Oven thermometer: See: A word on ovens (page 13). An oven thermometer is cheap, you can find one at a hardware store, and it tells you the most accurate temperature of your oven. Buy one, keep it in your oven, and never guess again.

Dough scraper: This is the first tool I ever formed an emotional attachment to and it is forever linked in my brain with learning how to make desserts. My boss, Ron Mendoza, gave me one during my first week on the job and told me to never lose it. In an effort to keep track of it, we dyed it a neon pink color and I treasured it forever and ever, until I lost it some weeks later. Rinse-and-repeat with several more dough scrapers throughout my life, but now that I'm mostly in one place, I lose them with slightly less frequency. I use them to scrape the batter from a bowl, to transfer chopped nuts from cutting board to bowl, scrape pie dough off the counter, cut scones in half, you name it. Beyond baking, I also use it as an extension of my hand for all things savory—moving chopped onions, garlic, and herbs from one place to another, transferring roasted vegetables from sheet pan to plate, etc.

Food processor: For the most part, many things you can use a food processor for you can do by hand, but crushing entire bags of cookies for a crust or grinding nuts to a powder fine enough to bake with is much easier in a food processor. If you don't want to splurge on a stand mixer or electric mixer, it's also possible to do things like make cookie dough in a food processor (considerably more affordable), another reason it's worth the shelf space.

Stand mixer/electric mixer: I'm placing these two things together in the same category because usually they are interchangeable, although my allegiance lies with the stand mixer for its strength and efficiency (conversely, a handheld electric mixer is smaller and costs less, so I see both sides). Sadly, some things can't be made by hand—or, rather, made by hand, the recipe simply won't yield the same result. As a person who hates to hear that, I hate to say it even more. That said, if you don't have an electric or stand mixer, there is still plenty (a majority, even) for you in this book.

pies, tarts, galettes

I am not trying to hide that out of all the desserts that exist, pies, tarts, and galettes are my favorite (this is the first and longest chapter in this book about desserts). When I think of dessert as a general concept, I think first and foremost of something that would live here in this chapter: a lightly salted, crunchy, flaky, or crumbly crust filled with sweet-tart filling, creamy or fruit-forward, or occasionally a more adult-feeling bittersweet chocolate. The balance and contrast of exterior textures and interior flavors in one slice really "do it all" for me.

Aesthetically, they have a charming rusticness to them, which only accentuates their personality (versus something like, say, cake, where imperfections are more likely to be interpreted as a mistake). I would even say quirkiness is a prerequisite of their appeal.

It's true that pies, tarts, and galettes are a process, often involving multiple steps, longish bake, or chill times—but are by no means the most complicated. Nearly all the recipes in this chapter can be done by hand with little to no special equipment.

While some of the recipes may ask you to make a pie crust, chill it, then roll it out, plenty also just ask you to smash a bunch of cookies in a bag, mix with butter, and press it into a pan or pie plate. Some may suggest you make caramel, then turn it onto a custard to bake until set just-so, but others may only tell you it's fine to toss some fruit with some sugar, throw it into your crust, and bake for a small eternity. Plus, once they're done, they're done, great for anyone who loves a "do ahead." Perfect little parcels waiting to be sliced and loved.

simple fruit tart

Makes one 9-inch tart

For the crust

1⅓ cups/200g all-purpose flour

⅔ cup/80g powdered sugar

1½ teaspoons/6g kosher salt

1½ sticks/6 ounces/170g unsalted butter, melted and cooled slightly

For assembly

Vanilla Pastry Cream (page 158), cooled

½ pound/225g assorted fresh red fruits (raspberries, strawberries, currants, boysenberries), halved or sliced according to shape and size, OR any assortment of delicious, roasted fruits (see page 217 for inspiration)

Eat with
A hunk of salty cheese and sliced cured meats on a lovely little picnic.

Do ahead
The shortbread crust can be baked 2 days ahead, stored wrapped at room temperature. The tart itself can be made 2 days ahead but can get a little soggy after that. Store it wrapped and refrigerated. Serve chilled.

I love this basic, elegant, classy tart. It's reserved and restrained, it's prim and proper, it's creamy and delicious. It's also one of the more flexible desserts in this book, and if you're the type of baker who loves to arrange your fruit like a gorgeous mosaic, well, this recipe is for you. Three distinct components, comprising an easy shortbread-like press-in crust, silky vanilla custard, and whatever fruit strikes you as most lovely when it comes time to makes this tart. Since the crust and custard already give you something so fantastic, whatever you choose to top it with is truly a cherry on top, no pun intended (unless you're using cherries, then definitely pun intended).

1   **Make the crust:** Preheat the oven to 350°F.

2   In a medium bowl, combine the flour, powdered sugar, and salt. Using your fingers, incorporate the melted butter until you've got a crumbly, Play-Doh-like textured dough. Resist the urge to knead the dough, as you don't want to develop any gluten (that's how the crust shrinks on you).

3   Press the dough into a 9-inch tart pan with a removable bottom or a 9-inch springform pan and use the tines of a fork or the tip of a knife to lightly prick the top all over (to allow steam to escape as it bakes).

4   Bake until the bottom of the crust is golden brown, and the edges are the color of a nicely golden shortbread cookie, 18–20 minutes (this tart does not get baked again, so this is your chance to fully bake through). Remove from the oven and let cool completely.

5   **Assemble the tart:** Once the tart shell is cooled, whisk the vanilla pastry cream until it's totally smooth (it will look firm, lumpy, and cottage cheese-like until it smooths out and comes together, looking like the gorgeous, smooth pudding it once was). Spread this into the tart shell.

6   Top with fruit of your choosing, but for the simplest version, use lovely, uncooked berries, preferably all from the same color family. Strawberries thinly sliced crosswise to expose their circular core, raspberries either left whole or cut in half, red currants if you can find them, you get the idea.

7   Refrigerate for 1 hour or so to set and chill before slicing.

caramelized vanilla custard tart

Makes one 9-inch tart

All-purpose flour, for dusting

1 disc The Only Pie Crust
(page 280)

Vanilla Pastry Cream (page 158)

Eat with
A nice glass of sherry, maybe a
little fresh fruit.

Do ahead
The tart shell can be baked
2 days ahead of time, stored
wrapped tightly at room
temperature.

Note
I find the custard browns more
evenly and quicker when the
pastry cream is NOT chilled,
but poured into the crust while
still hot, or at least warm.

There's a dessert called a Parisian Custard Tart, which is a flaky crust (often puff pastry) baked in a tall mold, filled with pastry cream, and baked till blackened. It's almost like a sweet quiche. There's a dessert called a Portuguese Egg Custard Tart, similar to the above but made in small, individual tart pans, with a slightly softer, sweeter custard, baked hot so that it browns and blackens in spots. To add to the collection, there's a Hong Kong–style Egg Custard Tart, similar to the aforementioned but with a glossy, pale finish and a more tender type of crust. Point being: Custard (milk or cream sweetened with sugar and thickened with eggs) baked into a buttery shell (puff pastry, short crust, etc.) is a divine thing that many people have figured out how to enjoy in many thicknesses and textures.

This is my version, combining elements of all of the above—a pie crust (for sturdiness AND flakiness) and a versatile pastry cream that's just as good eaten on its own like pudding as it is baked into a shell to get so dark you swear you've burned it (you haven't). It's shallow rather than thick, for an optimal crust-to-filling ratio with a not-too-sweet finish.

1 Preheat the oven to 350°F.

2 On a lightly floured work surface, roll the dough out to a rough round about 14 inches in diameter. Gently drape the dough into a 9-inch tart pan with removable bottom or pie plate (not deep-dish). Line the bottom and sides with the dough, pressing up the sides, trimming any excess overhang. Prick all over with a fork or tip of a knife. Line with parchment paper and fill with pie weights or dried beans.

3 Bake until golden brown on the sides and on the bottom (this is your chance to crisp up the bottom!), 20–25 minutes. Remove it from the oven.

4 Increase the oven temperature to 450°F.

5 Fill the shell with the pastry cream, smoothing the top, and bake until the top starts to caramelize to the point of near blackening, 15–25 minutes.

6 Let cool at room temperature before slicing (it's also great chilled).

perfect tangy chocolate tart

Makes one 9-inch tart

For the crust

¾ cup/110g all-purpose flour

¼ cup/28g unsweetened cocoa powder

⅓ cup/40g powdered sugar

½ teaspoon/2g kosher salt

1 stick/4 ounces/115g unsalted butter, melted

For the filling

8 ounces/226g bittersweet chocolate (68%–80% cacao)

4 ounces/114g milk chocolate (or more bittersweet chocolate)

Pinch of kosher salt

⅔ cup/160g heavy cream

⅓ cup/110g honey

1 cup/220g sour cream

Flaky sea salt

Eat with
A bowl of tangerines for peeling and nibbling in-between bites. A good amaro. A bowl of vanilla ice cream.

Do ahead
The cocoa crust can be made 3 days ahead, wrapped tightly, stored at room temperature. The tart itself can be made 3 days ahead, wrapped tightly and refrigerated.

If you, like me, trend toward fruit and vanilla over chocolate, I feel confident you could still fall in love with this perfectly basic, straightforward, yet completely above average chocolate tart. This one is easy to execute, flawless each and every time, doable by even those who have never so much as melted chocolate, let alone dared make a chocolate tart. If you scanned the ingredients and thought "milk chocolate? I'd never," then consider this my plea, my ask-on-hands-and-knees, to please, please trust me here and try it. I trust you'll find it plenty chocolaty and even more well-balanced than your typical tart. Oh, and not that you would, but please don't skimp on the salt.

1 **Make the crust:** Preheat the oven to 350°F. In a medium bowl, combine the flour, cocoa powder, powdered sugar, and kosher salt. Drizzle in the melted butter and mix until well combined (it'll have a sort of Play-Doh-type texture). Press this into the bottom and up the sides of a 9-inch tart pan with a removable bottom (or you can use a 9-inch pie plate or springform pan), using a measuring cup or your hands to flatten it and make sure it's all packed and even.

2 Bake until it's completely baked through and gone from dark brown and shiny to a lighter dark brown and matte, 15–20 minutes. (It can be difficult to tell when this is done because it's already brown. Test by pressing the center: it should be firm and opaque, not squishy or greasy-looking.) Remove from the oven and let cool completely.

3 **Make the filling:** In a heatproof medium bowl, combine the dark and milk chocolates and kosher salt. Set aside.

4 In a small saucepan, heat the cream and honey over medium heat. Once it starts to simmer, remove it from the heat (do not let it boil) and pour it over the chocolate. Let it sit for a minute or two to melt the chocolate, then, using a spatula, mix until well blended and no pieces of chocolate remain (you can whisk, but be cautious of air bubbles).

5 Stir in the sour cream and mix until it looks thick, glossy, and emulsified. Immediately pour the filling into the cooled crust and smooth the top. Sprinkle with flaky salt and refrigerate. Let chill at least 1 hour before slicing.

caramelized maple tart

Makes one 9-inch tart

For the crust

1⅓ cups/200g all-purpose flour

⅔ cup/80g powdered sugar

1½ teaspoons/6g kosher salt

1½ sticks/6 ounces/170g unsalted butter, melted and cooled slightly

For the filling

½ cup maple syrup

¼ teaspoon ground cinnamon (optional)

1 cup/230g heavy cream

1 large egg

1 large egg yolk

1 tablespoon/8g cornstarch

½ teaspoon/2g kosher salt

For serving

Whipped cream

Maple syrup (optional)

Flaky sea salt

Eat with
Thanksgiving dinner, a fire, some sort of cable-knit sweater.

Do ahead
The tart can be made 5 days ahead, stored wrapped and refrigerated.

I may be speaking to an audience of one (it's me), but if you have ever wanted a pumpkin pie to be something else, like, say, something without pumpkin, then I might suggest this pie. It's pumpkin-free, but thanks to deep, rich maple flavor and a respectful amount of cinnamon, it still feels autumnal enough to stand in for a pumpkin pie.

Asking you to boil maple syrup in a pot until it reduces so far that it starts to caramelize might feel like a wild ask, but I know you're going to appreciate the concentrated flavor without the tooth-aching sweetness (reducing the syrup concentrates the flavor and sugar content, so you need less of it in the filling). While it might be a challenge to tell when, exactly, it's caramelized (it starts off as an amber color, so), you will be able to smell it (it'll smell like caramel), and see it (the bubbles going from fast and furious to thick and luxuriously slow).

1   **Make the crust:** Preheat the oven to 350°F.

2   In a medium bowl, combine the flour, powdered sugar, and salt. Using your fingers, incorporate the melted butter until you've got a crumbly, Play-Doh-like textured dough. Resist the urge to knead the dough, you do not want to develop any gluten in this (that's when you get a crust that shrinks on you).

3   Press the dough into a 9-inch tart pan with a removable bottom or a 9-inch springform pan and use the tines of a fork or the tip of a knife to lightly prick the top all over to allow steam to escape as it bakes (this prevents bubbles).

4   Bake the crust until the bottom is lightly golden brown and the top goes from shiny to opaque (a good telltale that it's baked through), 15–18 minutes (it will get baked again with the filling, so don't worry too much about the edges being totally golden brown). Remove from the oven and let cool completely. Leave the oven on.

5   **Make the filling:** In a small pot, bring the maple syrup to a boil over medium heat and continue to cook until the color goes from pale golden brown with lots of small, furious bubbles to dark golden brown with larger, slower bubbles, 8–10 minutes. What we're doing here is evaporating the water in the maple syrup to concentrate the flavors and caramelize the sugars. The smell should never be that of "caramel" but more of "the most intense maple syrup you've ever smelled," like if maple syrup was a candy or a scratch-and-sniff sticker (do they still make those?).

6   Once the maple syrup has reached the desired caramelized stage, add the cinnamon (if using) and slowly whisk in the heavy cream, letting it bubble up as you add it in stages so the maple syrup doesn't seize up and harden. Remove from heat and set aside.

7   In a medium bowl, whisk together the whole egg, egg yolk, cornstarch, and salt. Using a ladle or measuring cup, add a generous ½ cup pour of the maple mixture to the egg mixture while whisking to blend. Add another ½ cup, continuing to whisk. Add the remaining maple mixture to the bowl with the eggs, whisking to blend.

8   Pour the maple mixture into the prebaked crust. Return to the oven and bake until the custard is set, no longer jiggling in the center, and has a nice shiny top, 35–40 minutes.

9   **To serve:** Let cool completely. Serve topped with whipped cream, perhaps some more maple syrup, and a bit of flaky salt.

blueberry cornmeal shortbread tart

Makes one 9-inch tart

For the crust and topping

1½ cups/220g all-purpose flour

⅓ cup/55g medium-grind cornmeal

⅓ cup/40g powdered sugar

¼ cup/50g light brown sugar

1 teaspoon/4g baking powder

1 teaspoon/4g kosher salt

1½ sticks/6 ounces/170g unsalted butter, melted and cooled slightly

For the filling

1 pound/455g blueberries or a combination of blueberries, blackberries, and raspberries

½ cup/110g light brown sugar

2 tablespoons/30g apple cider vinegar or fresh lemon juice

2 tablespoons/20g all-purpose flour

Pinch of kosher salt

Eat with
Vanilla ice cream would be too obvious, but I don't care.

Do ahead
Tart can be baked 4 days ahead, stored wrapped in plastic at room temperature, or refrigerated.

If you told me I could never bake a pie or a galette ever again but I could have this tart—that would be fine by me, because this tart does everything a pie or galette should do, almost better. It's crunchy, it's buttery, and it gorgeously celebrates your summertime fruit with minimal interference, low effort, and high reward. No crust to chill, no cake batter to second-guess, only one cornmeal-laced streusel-y topping that also functions as the crust (two birds, one very golden delicious stone). While I truly believe blueberries to be The Chosen Ones here (no cutting required, excellent juiciness, high pectin content for proper thickening), you should feel open to mixing your berries.

This tart is a prime candidate for baking in "whatever you have around." Tart pan, pie plate, square baking dish. It is also easily doubled to make in a 9 × 13-inch pan for more of a "bar" and less of a "tart."

1 **Make the crust and topping:** Preheat the oven to 350°F. In a medium bowl, whisk together the flour, cornmeal, powdered sugar, brown sugar, baking powder, and salt. Add the melted butter, then use your hands or a wooden spoon to combine the ingredients until a coarse little dough comes together, with no obviously dry spots.

2 Press three-quarters of the cornmeal mixture into a 9-inch tart pan with a removable bottom. (Alternatively, use a 9-inch round cake pan, 9-inch springform pan, or an 8 × 8-inch pan lined with parchment.) Make sure the mixture is evenly pressed on the bottom and about ½ inch up the sides. (Using something like the bottom of a measuring cup will be helpful.) Place the tart shell on a sheet pan and pop it (and the remaining cornmeal mixture) into the fridge while you prepare the filling.

3 **Make the filling:** In a medium bowl, toss the blueberries, brown sugar, vinegar, flour, and salt together. Pour the fruit into the crust. Crumble the remaining cornmeal mixture over the blueberries, pressing the mixture together into large clumps as you go, as you would with a crisp or coffeecake topping (it won't cover the top entirely; just a nice sporadic covering, to allow the blueberries and their juices to poke through).

4 Bake until the filling is bubbling, and the crust and top are nicely browned, 50–55 minutes. Let the tart cool completely before serving.

how to

how to galette

Pull your chilled **pie dough** (page 280) from the fridge. Start with the dough on a lightly floured piece of parchment paper so you can easily transport that to the rimmed baking sheet, rather than trying to transport the rolled dough or the unbaked galette, which can end in tears (both tears from the eyes and tears in the dough).

Decide your shape. I like to think that the shape of the fruit determines the shape of the galette, but you should not feel beholden to a "traditional shape." Make one up! This is your galette.

Starting at the center, roll it thinner than you think, so the crust can really get crispy (thicker crust = doughier crust), aiming for a circle about 13 inches in diameter. Dust the top lightly with **flour** and flip the whole crust over to prevent sticking, then continue to roll. Should your crust feel especially dry, and you notice cracking, give it a second on the counter to soften. You can also patch up any holes or egregious tears with dough from the perimeter. If it feels warm and sticky, pop it into the fridge to chill a bit before continuing.

Try not to fuss too much over finessing the edges—craggly, irregular bits on the perimeter are what make the finished product beautiful and unique. Put the crust on a baking sheet and in the fridge until you're ready to add the fruit.

Regarding fruit, there are no real wrong answers here. I like to appreciate one fruit at a time, but if you're into the mélange, go for it. Strawberries, blueberries, plums, peaches, nectarines, and apricots all get a turn on my galette summer stage, and in the fall, I am a sucker for apples, simple and tart.

For one galette, you'll need more fruit than you think, **about 1 full pound (450g) of berries** (if using strawberries, cut them in half or into quarters if large) **or 1¼ pounds (560g) stone fruit or apples**, sliced and pitted. Toss the fruit with about **½ cup (100g) sugar** and **2 tablespoons (15g) cornstarch** (you can use flour in a pinch, but I feel like it makes for a gummier texture and cloudier appearance). For a thrill, add something fun like citrus zest. **Add the juice of whatever fruit you just zested** (or if you didn't zest, a teeny splash of apple cider vinegar or red/white wine vinegar) and toss the fruit until it's all glossy and well coated. A small **pinch of salt** will do you many favors.

Crack **an egg** into a small bowl and whisk it with a little water to loosen it up. This is your egg wash and is the trick to that very golden, extremely lovely-looking crust. Even the most buttery of pie crusts shan't shine without it. (If you don't have/don't eat egg, a buttermilk, heavy cream, or milk wash will do the trick.)

Plop the fruit onto the dough, letting it pile on top of each other, leaving at least a 2-inch border. Gently but not preciously, fold the edges up and a little onto the fruit, covering by an inch or two, overlapping as you need. The deepest of the craggly edges of the crust are where a lot of juices will escape to (not that there's anything wrong with that), but to limit the outpouring of juices, make sure the cracks aren't too deep—if they are, use some extra dough where there is some to spare and patch up the cracks like the pie mason you are.

Using a clean paintbrush you got at Michaels or a hardware store (or maybe just use your fingers), brush the dough with the egg wash and sprinkle the whole unbaked galette with **granulated sugar or demerara/sugar in the raw/turbinado** if you have it (regular brown sugar kind of just melts and clumps onto the crust).

Bake this new friend at 375°F for 65 to 75 minutes (yes, a long time). The crust should be deeply browned like a good croissant and feel strong when you tap on it (go ahead, tap it, it should sound almost hollow). If it feels like it's getting dark, but the crust isn't yet baked through, reduce the temperature to 350°F and continue to bake.

The juices will have likely bubbled up and over the crust in places, which will look nice. If a leak has somehow sprung while baking, do not panic, do not self-flagellate; this is not a failure. Above all: Do not try to fix it while it's in the oven—let nature run its course. Those juices may char to carbon on the sheet pan, and someone will ask if something is burning. "Yes, but it's fine! It'll soak off!" you can say.

Let the galette cool slightly to give the juices a chance to settle and thicken up before slicing. You can transfer it to a wire baking rack if you have one; otherwise, just let it hang out on that sheet tray that may take a while to clean.

Slice and eat the galette. It tastes good, right? You kind of like those charred, very caramelized bits around the edges, right? I'm glad, that was on purpose, you'll tell yourself. This is "a caramelized galette!" No matter the outcome, take pride in knowing this is your galette. There are many like it, but this one is yours.

tiny strawberry galettes

Makes 8 galettes

All-purpose flour, for dusting

2 discs The Only Pie Crust (page 280)

1½ pounds/680g strawberries, hulled and quartered (or chopped if especially large)

3 tablespoons/30g cornstarch

⅓ cup/70g sugar, plus more for sprinkling

2 tablespoons/30g fresh lemon or lime juice

½ teaspoon rose water or orange blossom water (optional)

1 large egg

Finely chopped pistachios, pecans, almonds, or hazelnuts (optional)

Eat with
A scoop of any ice cream you'd want to eat with strawberries.

Do ahead
Tiny galettes are great made in advance and great for travel. They'll last at least 2 days, tightly wrapped and stored at room temperature.

Note
For those lacking in the perfectly ripe, juicy berry department, these galettes will still produce something delicious with even subpar fruit (again: baking is magic). Other fruits to consider are rhubarb (unpeeled, cut into 3-inch-ish pieces) or raspberries (as is).

Not all fruit is interesting enough to carry a small handheld galette on its own without the need for additional flavors or faffing, but in-season strawberries absolutely are. The perfectly juicy little orbs transform in the oven; juices bubble up and evaporate, concentrating flavors, while the texture and shape stay intact, firming up not unlike a semi-leathery sun-dried tomato. What comes out is a better strawberry than what went in, baked inside a personalized flaky, caramelized crust.

1   Preheat the oven to 375°F. Line two baking sheets with parchment paper.

2   On a lightly floured work surface, roll each disc of dough out to about 14 inches in diameter, give or take; make sure that the dough is evenly rolled, with no parts thicker or thinner than the other, even if that means an uneven circular shape. Cut each dough round into 4 even quarters and transfer to the lined baking sheets. Refrigerate while you prepare the filling.

3   In a medium bowl, combine the strawberries, cornstarch, sugar, lemon juice, and rose water (if using). Toss once or twice to combine.

4   Remove the dough from the fridge. Working with one at a time, remove a piece of dough from the lined baking sheet. Spoon strawberry mixture in the center of the dough, leaving about a 1-inch border of dough, piling it higher rather than spreading wider. Fold up the edges just over the edge of the fruit, making more of an imperfect circular shape rather than reinforcing the triangle shape from whence it came. If you notice any large tears or cracks, simply patch them up by pressing the dough back together until sealed. Return each small galette to a lined baking sheet.

5   Whisk the egg with a teaspoon of water and brush the edges of the crust with the egg wash. Sprinkle with any finely chopped nuts you may be using (if you're using) over the crust, followed by a nice dusting of sugar.

6   Bake, rotating the baking sheets once or twice until the crust of the small galettes is deeply browned like a graham cracker and the filling is bubbling, looking thick and shiny like melted fruit leather, 35–40 minutes. Remove from the oven and let cool before eating.

Note

Using fresh or dried flowers is a lovely thing to do for decor, but even better when they can impart actual flavor. Chamomile, which is in season in many places from early June to mid-August, has a delicately floral, almost grassy scent and pairs exceptionally well with stone fruit. Fresh or dried work here (I typically rip open a high-quality tea bag), but the potency is concentrated when dried.

peaches and cream galette

Makes one 10-inch galette

All-purpose flour, for dusting

1 disc The Only Pie Crust
(page 280)

2 pounds/900g peaches,
nectarines, or apricots, unpeeled,
cut into slices about 1 inch thick

2 tablespoons fresh lemon or
lime juice

5-6 tablespoons sugar

⅓ cup sweetened
condensed milk

1 large egg

1 teaspoon dried chamomile
or 1 tablespoon fresh (optional;
see Note, opposite)

Eat with
Whipped cream, 50/50 (Tangy
Whipped Cream, page 279),
or vanilla ice cream.

Do ahead
The galette is best eaten the day
of, but will definitely last a day or
two, stored at room temperature,
loosely covered with foil or
plastic wrap. You can always
rewarm in a 375°F oven if you like,
but I almost prefer galettes at
room temperature.

This will not be the only time peaches and cream makes an appearance in this book (see Naked Peaches, page 228), and that's because I can't get enough of the combination. This one is a bit less literal: The "cream" here is from a generous pour of sweetened condensed milk, which while not technically cream, is still arguably creamy. As the peaches bake inside their perfect crust, the sweetened condensed milk bubbles up around the edges and into the nooks, caramelizing in the crannies and crevices created by the uneven wedges of peach. The chamomile is optional, but if you can get it (fresh is often in season while peaches are; dried is a nice substitute), it's a subtle but very gorgeous flavor that was truly born to be eaten with peaches and cream.

1 Preheat the oven to 375°F. Line a baking sheet with parchment paper.

2 On a lightly floured work surface, roll the dough out to a 13–14-inch round and transfer to the lined baking sheet.

3 Arrange the peach slices in the center of the dough, letting the slices pile on top of each other (or, if you're more of a concentric circle/meticulous pattern kind of person, go ahead), leaving a 2-inch border of dough all around. Gently toss the peaches with lemon juice and 2 tablespoons of the sugar.

4 Drizzle the sweetened condensed milk over the peaches, letting it pool and gather in the nooks and crannies. Fold the crust up over the peaches by about 2 inches, crimping/overlapping the dough at 1- or 2-inch intervals to create a good seal for all the juiciness to come.

5 In a small bowl, whisk the egg with 1 teaspoon or so of water and use that to brush onto the crust. Sprinkle the whole galette (fruit and crust) with 3–4 tablespoons more sugar for juicier fruit and an extra crunchy/craggly/golden crust.

6 Bake, rotating the baking sheet front to back once, until the crust is deeply golden brown and baked through, the peaches are juicy, tender, and bubbling with excitement, 50–55 minutes. While still warm, sprinkle with chamomile, if using. Let cool completely before slicing and serving with the creamy thing of your choosing (or just as is is lovely, too).

sugar plum galette with halva

Makes one 10-inch galette

All-purpose flour, for dusting

1 disc The Only Pie Crust
(page 280) or Whole Wheat Pie
Crust (page 281)

2 pounds/910g plums or apricots,
halved through the stem end

⅓ cup/70g demerara or
granulated sugar, plus more
for sprinkling

3½ ounces/100g halva or almond
paste, crumbled (about ¾ cup)

1 large egg

1 tablespoon fresh thyme leaves,
optional

Eat with
Vanilla ice cream is always a "yes"
from me, but plums specifically
really do take a shine to other
flavors. This is an instance
where I would push for serving
an "alternative" ice cream,
something made with caramel,
honey, sesame, or nuts.

Do ahead
The galette is best eaten the day
of, but will definitely last a day or
two, stored at room temperature,
loosely covered with foil or
plastic wrap. You can always
rewarm in a 375°F oven if you like,
but I almost prefer galettes at
room temperature.

Halva can refer to myriad confections around the world, some semolina-based, others made from sesame, a pulverized nut, or some combination of all three. Some are cookie-like, some are small and candy-like. Here I am referring to the block of sweetened sesame paste that is sold by the hunk in many Middle Eastern and Jewish groceries.

The halva here is subtle, but adds a welcomed nutty flavor and tender texture on top of the flaky crust, and beneath the jammy fruit, lending it a not-*not* peanut butter and jelly quality. It's also lending its talents as a sweetener (meaning less granulated sugar on your fruit), and also providing something for those juices to sink into as the fruit bakes, which leaves you with a never-soggy bottom.

1   Preheat the oven to 375°F. Line a baking sheet with parchment paper.

2   On a lightly floured work surface, roll the dough out to a round-ish 13–14-inch round and transfer to the lined baking sheet.

3   In a medium bowl, toss the plums with the sugar until well coated. Scatter the halva onto the dough round, making sure to break up any aggressively large pieces, leaving a 2-inch border of dough all around. Top with the plums; I like to do a mix of cut-side up and cut-side down for a good distribution of juiciness and, of course, for looks.

4   Fold the crust up over the plums, overlapping slightly to create a good seal for all the juiciness to come.

5   Whisk your egg with a teaspoon or so of water and use that to brush the crust with the egg wash. Sprinkle the whole galette (the crust and the plums) with more sugar for juicier fruit and an extra crunchy/craggly/golden crust.

6   Bake, rotating the pan front to back once, until the crust is deeply golden brown and baked through, the plums are juicy, tender, and bubbling with excitement, 50–55 minutes. Remove from the oven and sprinkle with thyme, if using. Let cool completely before slicing.

deep-dish apple galette

Makes one deep, 9-inch galette

For the dough

3 cups/435g all-purpose flour

2 tablespoons/25g granulated sugar

1½ teaspoons/6g kosher salt

3 sticks/12 ounces/340g cold unsalted butter, cut into 1-inch pieces

1 tablespoon/15g apple cider vinegar

⅓ cup/80g ice water

For the filling

2½ pounds/1.13kg firm, tart baking apples, cored and thinly sliced (about 8 cups)

¾ cup/240g mild-flavored honey

½ cup/110g granulated sugar

2 tablespoons/18g all-purpose flour, plus more for dusting

1 tablespoon/15g apple cider vinegar or fresh lemon juice

1½ teaspoons ground cinnamon

I would argue that for all the fruits available to turn into a galette, the apple is the most well-behaved candidate. Rarely too juicy, a pleasant balance of sweet and tart but not too much of one or the other, it's just a kind of middle-of-the-road fruit that always tastes like itself. If you're picking up on some subtext that suggests I think apples are a little boring, well, you're right. But sometimes, I like boring. Sometimes, safe, reliable, and a little milquetoast is exactly what you want. Plus, that's what the honey and apple cider vinegar are there for—to keep things interesting.

Anyway, a deep-dish galette is just like a regular galette, except baked in a vessel that facilitates a . . . deep dish. Think tall. Think open-faced pie. As for the chosen vessel, a 9-inch springform pan really is what you want here—it has high sides that give the crust plenty of structure and support, plus the chance to have those extremely dramatic golden brown walls made of buttery crust. Of course, a deep-dish pie plate will work, and so will a cake pan! You could even bake this in a deep 9- or 10-inch cast-iron skillet—the choices are limitless.

The dough here is essentially the same as The Only Pie Crust (page 280), just with slightly different ratios to make exactly what you'll need for the deep-dish galette. You may have a bit of excess, but I figured in this case it was better to have too much rather than not enough.

1   **Make the dough:** In a large bowl, combine the flour, sugar, and kosher salt and use your hands to mix well.

2   Add the butter to the bowl and use your palms and fingertips to smash the pieces into the flour until you've got large, flat butter pieces that are evenly distributed throughout the flour. Pop the bowl into the freezer for 5 or so minutes.

3   In a measuring cup, combine the vinegar and ice water and drizzle it over the flour/butter mixture. Like you're running your hands through sand, deliberately yet delicately mix the water into the flour/butter mixture until it forms a shaggy clump. Resist the urge to add more water, knowing that as you further knead, it will become less dry.

Cooking spray, softened butter, or oil, for the pan

All-purpose flour, for dusting

1 large egg

3 tablespoons white sesame seeds (optional)

2 tablespoons sugar

Flaky sea salt

Vanilla ice cream, for serving

Eat with

I like deep-dish galettes for holidays, they're just so large and grand, they really do feel celebratory. I especially enjoy them for Rosh Hashanah and Thanksgiving, two times you might already to expect to see apples and honey together.

Do ahead

The dough can be made 5 days ahead, wrapped and refrigerated. The galette can and should be baked a day ahead, stored loosely covered at room temperature. If you like, you can bake it up to 2 days ahead, then wrap in foil and store in the refrigerator—it can be gently rewarmed in a 375°F oven to take the chill off.

4 Turn the dough out onto a work surface and use your palms to knead it lightly until the shaggy clump transforms into a slightly less shaggy mass of dough. (It should still be relatively shaggy.) Pat the dough into a disc about 1 inch thick, rotating it to create a nice round. Wrap in plastic or place in a resealable plastic bag and chill until firm, at least 2 hours.

5 Preheat the oven to 375°F. Remove the dough from the refrigerator and let it soften slightly at room temperature, about 10 minutes or so.

6 **Meanwhile, make the filling:** In a large bowl, combine the apples, honey, sugar, the 2 tablespoons flour, the vinegar, and cinnamon. Toss the ingredients so every slice of apple is evenly coated.

7 **To assemble:** Lightly grease a 9-inch springform pan or a 9-inch deep-dish pie plate. On a lightly floured work surface, roll the dough out to a round about 18 inches in diameter. Transfer the dough to the prepared pan, letting it slump to meet the bottom of the pan and letting the overhang remain.

8 Transfer the apple mixture and any juices that have accumulated to the crust. Drape the excess dough over the filling, covering the apples by 1½–2 inches. (Feel free to trim any dough that feels truly excessive.)

9 Whisk the egg with a teaspoon of water and use it to brush the exposed crust. Sprinkle with sesame seeds (if using), the sugar, and a little flaky salt.

10 Place the galette on a sheet pan (for easy cleanup should anything bubble over) and bake until the crust is deeply golden brown (about the color of a well-baked croissant), the apples are tender, and the juices are bubbling and thickened, 1 hour 5 minutes to 1 hour 15 minutes.

11 Let the galette cool completely (at least 2 hours) before slicing and eating, preferably with lots of ice cream.

what I love about baking

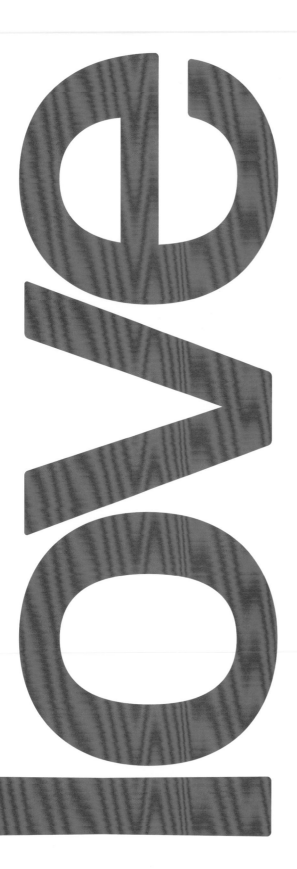

I love separating the egg yolks from the white with my bare hands and stacking the eggshells in the paper crate they came in. I love the smell, taste, look, experience of making browned butter, it is the first food I fell in romantic love with. I love the sense of accomplishment after I pull something out of the oven even if I haven't done a single other thing that day. I love how baking makes me feel like a wizard and a scientist and a magician. I love to contradict my penchant for chaos with the precision of baking. I love licking the bowls where there was once raw cake batter. I love eating the unbaked pie dough before it becomes a pie. I love celebrating fruit. I love celebrating butter. I love eating shavings of cold butter. I love ripening bananas for banana bread in my window, hanging them like a plant. I love finding whipped cream in my hair after whipping it by hand. I love mundane, repetitive tasks like pitting cherries.

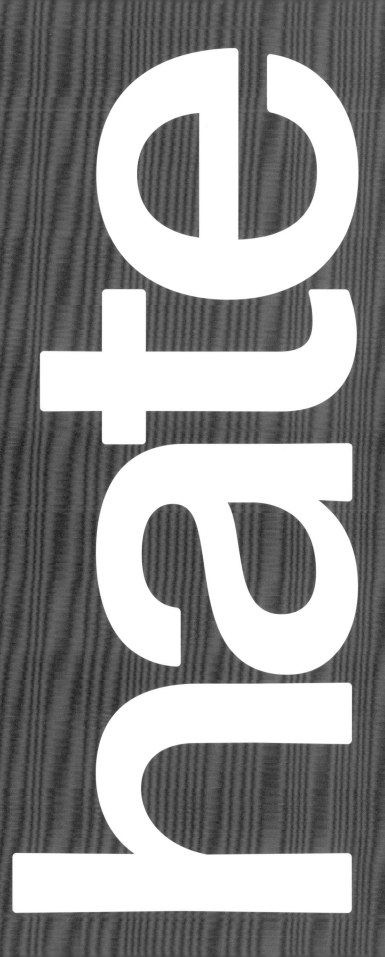

what I hate about baking

I hate how many bowls I have to clean. I hate the lack of standardized measurements. I hate needing special equipment. I hate how long it takes for cookie dough to chill before you can bake it. I hate how long it takes pies to bake. I hate how long it takes cake to cool down before you can eat. I hate waiting. I hate that the fruit is the best at the hottest time of year because then you have to turn your oven on to bake something, and I hate that, too. I hate when I mess up and feel like I just wasted hours of my life. I hate how much planning most desserts take because I'm horrible at planning. I hate how long it takes for butter to actually and properly come to room temperature. I hate finding frosting in my hair after frosting a cake. I hate messy, eternal tasks like pitting cherries.

sour cherry crumble pie

Makes one 9-inch pie

All-purpose flour, for dusting

1 disc The Only Pie Crust
(page 280)

Egg wash: 1 large egg, beaten

8 cups/3 pounds/1.35kg pitted
sour cherries* (from about
3½ pounds/1.6kg unpitted)

¾ cup/165g sugar

⅓ cup/40g cornstarch

Grated zest and juice of 2 limes
or 1 lemon

Freshly ground black pepper

Salted Nutty Crumble (page 290),
unbaked

Flaky sea salt

*Sweet cherries are not a
substitute.

Eat with
Cold heavy cream, vanilla ice
cream, or 50/50 (Tangy Whipped
Cream, page 279).

Do ahead
Pie can and should be baked
a day ahead, stored loosely
covered at room temperature.
It will last a few days at room
temperature or in the fridge.

Note
To turn this into a double-crust pie,
ditch the crumble and follow the
instructions for the Double Crust
Fruit Pie on page 59—and, yes,
it will have to bake just as long!

Very few of you will get to bake this pie with fresh sour cherries because fresh sour cherries are, by and large, not easy to find. Short season, limited growing areas, etc. So what's it doing in this book? Because it's my favorite fruit pie, a true icon of the pie world. The lightly salted, nutty, toasted almond topping with enough butter and sugar to bind, the juicy cherries that remind you of sour candy, the flaky pie crust supporting it all—it simply can't be beat.

If you find fresh sour cherries hard to come by, frozen can be found on the internet (make jam with the extras—you can seemingly only buy a LOT at a time).

1 Preheat the oven to 375°F. Line a sheet pan with foil.

2 On a lightly floured work surface, roll out the dough to a diameter of about 12 inches. Fit the dough into a 9-inch pie plate, letting it hang over the sides. Trim the edges so you've got 1½–2 inches overhang. Fold the excess dough onto the lip of the pie plate, then crimp the crust with the style of your choosing—thumb and forefinger, tines of a fork, etc.

3 Whisk the egg with a teaspoon of water and brush the edges of the crust with the egg wash. Place the pie plate on the lined sheet pan and set aside.

4 In a medium bowl, combine the cherries, sugar, cornstarch, lime zest, lime juice, and a few good grinds of black pepper. Toss to dissolve the sugar and cornstarch (the cornstarch can be stubborn, so mix, mix, mix).

5 Transfer the cherry mixture to the pie shell (all the cherries, all their juices, everybody in). Sprinkle the salted nutty crumble on in one nice, even layer. Sprinkle with flaky salt and another good grind of pepper.

6 Place the pie in the oven and bake, rotating the pie plate front to back once, until the crust is golden brown and baked through, the topping is deeply crisped, and the juices of the cherries have gone from thin and watery to thick and juicy, 1 hour 45 minutes to 2 hours. This, sadly, is not a typo.

7 Remove the pie from the oven and let it cool completely, at least 8 hours, or else it will be too runny when you slice it.

tangy buttermilk pie

10 graham crackers/150g

¾ cup/165g sugar,
plus 2 tablespoons/28g

6 tablespoons/3 ounces/85g
unsalted butter, melted

1¼ cup/300g buttermilk

¼ cup/60g distilled white vinegar

4 large eggs

2 tablespoons/20g cornstarch

Pinch of kosher salt

1 cup/220g sour cream

Eat with
A glass of wine or a few hunks of
very dark chocolate.

Do ahead
Tart can be made 2 days ahead
but can get a little soggy after
that. Store it wrapped and
refrigerated and serve chilled.

This is a sort of "Depression Era"–style dessert, meaning it's made from mostly pantry staples and also that it makes you feel better when you're depressed. Just kidding about that last part, unless you believe in the power of positive thinking, and then this pie can do anything.

Joking aside, this pie, in all its humble basicness, is truly spectacular. The custard, tasting of the tangiest buttermilk, melts into the buttery, salty crust, creating a mysterious middle layer: softer than the crunchy base and more substantive than the silky top layer, behaving almost like the lemon bar of your dreams (except there's no lemon). How buttermilk, vinegar, and graham crackers could create something so phenomenal, I simply don't know.

1   Preheat the oven to 325°F. Crush the crackers in a food processor or by hand (place them in a zip-top bag and crush with a rolling pin). In a medium bowl, mix them with 2 tablespoons/28g of the sugar. Pour in the melted butter and mix until you've got a wet-sand-like texture.

2   Press the graham cracker mixture into a 9-inch tart pan (or a 9-inch pie plate), making sure the sides are reinforced and packed tightly before focusing on the bottom (use the palm of your hand or the bottom of a measuring cup).

3   Bake the crust until it's golden brown on the edges, 10–15 minutes. It can be tough to tell since the crackers are already golden, but they'll have a noticeably toastier look. Remove it from the oven and set aside.

4   In a large bowl, whisk together the buttermilk, vinegar, remaining ¾ cup/165g sugar, and the eggs. Add the cornstarch and salt and whisk to combine. Gently pour the mixture into the parbaked crust (if a few little bits of crust pop up, that's okay).

5   Pop back into the oven and bake until the pie no longer jiggles in the center (tap it—it should be set, like a bowl of Jell-O), 15–20 minutes.

6   Let the pie cool completely. Transfer to the refrigerator and chill until totally set, at least 1 hour. When ready to serve, spread the sour cream all over the top of the pie in a gorgeous, thin layer. Slice and serve.

the allure of a double crust

Ah, the allure of a double-crust fruit pie. Peak season fruit behaving perfectly, cooking down to a jammy thickness inside a delightfully golden, flaky crust, neatly contained save for the one gorgeous drip that escaped out of the delicately cut vent on the top, a sneak peek of what's to come. Always juicy but never runny, sliceable but only barely, the just-set fruit quivering above the precariously thin sliver of dough.

All that sounds nice, doesn't it? Well, I only know it to exist as a fantasy. In my experience, a double-crust fruit pie will only break your heart.

The crimp you labored over baked and puffed to a barely recognizable blob. The left side of the crust slumped over mid-bake, exposing the insides, which caused the juices to leak onto the sheet tray, baking into a leathery sheet of juice so caramelized it borders on burnt that, yeah, you'll probably try to eat. The top looks nicely browned and golden, but the twee leaf-shaped design you painstakingly cut out of the top closed up in the oven and now looks like just one giant sheet of pie crust, no jammy juices peeking out just so, like the photo promised you they would.

So, now what? Despair? Not in this book, no. I can think about 739,275 other things worth worrying about, and "ugly pie" simply isn't one of them. To encourage this journey of radical pie acceptance, I leave you with a few pieces of advice:

Bake your pie longer than you think. Do I sound like a broken record? Bake your pie longer than you think! It will take so much longer than I'm suggesting you bake it to actually burn, and beyond that, what's the worst that could happen? The crust should be as brown as a graham cracker, not a shade lighter. During its time in the oven, the crust will go from pale and flabby to sturdy and tan, fulfilling its destiny as supremely crunchy and impossibly flaky. The juices of the fruit will go from runny and unruly to properly jammy and subtly tamed.

Let your pie rest until it's completely cooled to room temperature. I'm sorry to say that this can take as long as 8 hours, and no, this isn't a punishment. Most fruit pie will be too runny for nice, clean slices until it's totally cooled, which is why I almost always bake my pie the day before. And no, you cannot rush this by putting it in the refrigerator.

Manage your expectations. It would be very easy to make pie baking an allegory for life, in that our most crushing disappointments are directly proportioned to the expectations we set for them. The higher the something, the harder the fall, or whatever the saying is. Trust that no matter what it looks like, your pie will taste delicious. It is scientifically impossible for a crust made with butter, flour, sugar, and salt to taste bad when baked around good fruit tossed with sugar and lemon. If it falls apart, slumps, or spills, simply scoop it into a bowl and pretend it's a cobbler; cover it with a monstrous scoop of ice cream or a tall pile of whipped cream. Whatever you do, do not let the mysteries of baking and all that you cannot control ruin your day. After all, it is just pie, isn't it?

salted lemon cream pie

Makes one 9-inch pie

For the crust

8 ounces/225g vanilla wafers, graham crackers, or Biscoff

6 tablespoons/3 ounces/85g unsalted butter, melted

1 teaspoon/4g kosher salt

For the filling and topping

4 large egg yolks

1 (14-ounce/397g) can sweetened condensed milk

1¼ cups/295ml fresh lemon or Meyer lemon juice (about 6 lemons)

Kosher salt

1 cup/230ml heavy cream

¼ cup/30g powdered sugar

1 cup/220g sour cream

Eat with
A glass of sparkling wine or heavily lemon'd sparkling water.

Do ahead
This pie can be made 4 days ahead, stored loosely wrapped and refrigerated.

There are no meringues in this book. Before you get upset, please ask yourself, what is the meringue for? For whomst is the meringue? Raw egg whites (no flavor) and sugar (sweet) whipped together to give you something that looks pretty, except when you eat it, you're like, wait, did I just eat raw egg whites and sugar? Sure, the texture has the potential to be pleasant, but even on its best day it's not something I want to eat a ton of. And that's why a lemon meringue pie was never in the cards, but a lemon CREAM pie? Now, that is something I will die for. While the lemon (lean, acidic) merely tolerates meringue, it truly NEEDS the whipped cream (rich, fatty) to cut through, to round it out, to make the slice balanced and complete.

1 **Make the crust:** Preheat the oven to 350°F.

2 In a bowl, smash the vanilla wafers with your hands until you've got coarse crumbs, nothing larger than a lentil. (Alternatively, place the wafers in a resealable bag and crush with a rolling pin or use a food processor.) Mix with the melted butter and salt until you've got really moist crumbs, almost like wet sand. Press the crumbs into a 9-inch pie plate.

3 Bake until the crust starts to lightly brown around the edges, 12–15 minutes. Remove from the oven and set aside to cool. Leave the oven on.

4 **Make the filling:** In a large bowl, vigorously whisk the egg yolks until they're pale and fluffy, just a few minutes. Add the sweetened condensed milk and whisk a few more minutes, until the mixture is light and airy. Whisk in the lemon juice and a good pinch of salt.

5 Pour the filling into the partially baked crust and return it to the oven to bake until the center barely jiggles, another 30–35 minutes. FYI, the top should not brown, so keep an eye on it. Let the pie cool completely.

6 **Make the topping:** When it's time to serve this gorgeous pie, in a large bowl, with a whisk, whisk the cream and powdered sugar together until they've achieved medium peaks (this means that it will basically stand up on the ends of the whisk); you can also do this with an electric mixer. Whisk in the sour cream (no need to fold, the cream should hold up), then swirl that all over the top of the pie, as high or decoratively as you please.

black and blue hand pies

All-purpose flour, for dusting

2 discs The Only Pie Crust
(page 280)

1 pound/455g blueberries,
blackberries (halved lengthwise),
boysenberries, and/or mulberries

2 tablespoons/20g cornstarch

3 tablespoons/45g fresh lemon
or lime juice, plus grated zest
if you like

½ cup/110g granulated sugar

1 large egg

Demerara (or more granulated
sugar), for sprinkling

Eat with
Your hands, of course.

Do ahead
Hand pies are actually great
made in advance. They'll last at
least 2 days, wrapped and stored
at room temperature.

Hand pies are cute, they are convenient to travel with, and they have an excellent ratio of filling-to-crust. Instead of making these "Pop-Tart style," which is two crusts cut and fitted together and involves a level of precision I don't really have the patience for, I make them sort of turnover/empanada style, from one piece of dough folded onto itself. If you're a stickler for symmetry (then this isn't the book for you! Just kidding), then you can always punch out rounds to make even half-moons; but I think the following technique for creating the half-moon shape (as uneven as it may be) from a quartered round works great.

Like strawberries, blackberries and blueberries are extremely well suited for the smaller, more individualized experience of a tiny galette or hand pie. The seediness of the berries is pleasantly present but doesn't dominate, and since there's less fruit, they cook down quicker, eliminating the possibility of a runny pie (which almost always happens with a classic large double-crust pie, no matter the precautions taken to avoid it). Also, similarly to strawberries, they don't need much help being delicious—maybe just some citrus juice to augment their acidity and add a little je ne sais quoi.

1   Preheat the oven to 375°F. Line two baking sheets with parchment paper.

2   On a lightly floured work surface, roll each disc of dough out to about 14 inches in diameter, give or take; make sure that the dough is evenly rolled, with no parts thicker or thinner than the other, even if that means an uneven round shape. Cut each round into 4 even quarters and transfer to the lined baking sheets; refrigerate while you prepare the filling.

3   In a medium bowl, toss the berries with the cornstarch, lemon juice, and granulated sugar.

4 Remove the dough from the fridge. Working with one at a time, remove a piece of dough from the baking sheet. Spoon 2 tablespoons or so of the berry mixture into the center of the dough, perhaps a bit more toward the wide end (as opposed to the thin pointy end). Fold the pointy part of the dough up to meet the wide part, then fold the edges up onto themselves in a half-moon sort of shape (like an empanada). There is really no "wrong" way to do this, we are really just trying to make sure the fruit is sealed inside the crust. Press the edges so that everything is sealed inside. If you notice any large tears or cracks, simply patch them up by pressing the dough back together until sealed. Return the hand pie to its lined baking sheet.

5 When the first sheet is filled up, pop it into the fridge while you assemble the rest and await the bake.

6 Once all are assembled, whisk the egg with a teaspoon or so of water and use that to brush the outside of each pie, followed by a generous sprinkling of demerara sugar. Using a paring knife, cut 2–3 ample slits in the top of each hand pie (this is what allows the juices to escape, properly thickening the filling, so be generous!).

7 Pop the baking sheets into the oven and bake until each pie is gorgeously golden brown on the outside, the crust is baked through and firm, and the fruit inside is bubbling so furiously that it's creating little cascading drips of bright blue juice, thickening as it escapes, 25–30 minutes.

8 Let cool slightly before eating.

My favorite way to transport hand pies is to leave them clinging to the parchment they were baked on. I just rip the paper around them, using said parchment paper as a protective barrier during transit. Rustic and practical, like all my favorite things.

lemon shaker pie

Makes one 9-inch pie

2 Meyer or large regular lemons
(about 10 ounces/300g),
very thinly sliced and seeded

1¼ cups/260g sugar, plus more
for sprinkling

Kosher salt

4 large eggs

¼ cup/35g all-purpose flour,
plus more for dusting

2 discs The Only Pie Crust
(page 280)

Eat with
Thick clotted cream, mascarpone,
or crème fraîche.

Do ahead
This pie can be made 3 days
ahead, wrapped and stored at
room temperature or refrigerated.

Note
FYI, FWIW, this is maybe one of
the few pies that are better at
room temperature, even chilled.

From my lemon-obsessed point of view, I can confirm in a totally unbiased way that this is the best pie in the world. The name comes from the Shakers, a religious community who famously make use of the entirety of anything (an animal, a piece of wood, a whole lemon).

It's going to be sweet, of course, but it will also be bitter, complex, and tart because of the whole lemon, custardy because of the eggs, and a little salty, flaky, and crunchy because of the pie crust. It's also going to be easy and foolproof, perfectly set and golden brown each time, as if touched by some sort of baking angel. It's going to be everything you want a lemon bar to be but more and better.

1   Set aside a few lemon slices to put on top of the pie. In a medium bowl, combine the rest of the slices with the sugar and a good pinch of salt. Toss to coat and let sit at least 2 hours, up to 24 hours, refrigerated.

2   Preheat the oven to 350°F. Remove the lemons from the fridge and whisk in 3 of the eggs and the flour.

3   Dust a work surface with flour. Roll out each disc of dough to a round about 14 inches in diameter. Lay one into a 9-inch pie plate, letting the dough slump into the edges, leaving the overhang. Pour the filling into the crust.

4   In the other dough round, use a paring knife to cut in a few vents or simply prick all over with a fork. Drape it over the pie filling, then, using your thumb and forefinger, press the top and bottom crusts together to seal the two pieces together. Using the tines of a fork, press the crusts together onto the pie plate, creating an even tighter seal. Then, using a knife or scissors, trim any excessive overhang.

5   In a small bowl, whisk the remaining egg and a teaspoon or so of water together. Brush the pie all over with the egg wash and arrange the reserved lemon slices on top. Sprinkle the whole thing with sugar.

6   Bake until the crust is deeply golden and evenly browned, 1 hour 10 minutes to 1 hour 20 minutes. Let cool at least 2 hours before serving.

savories

caramelized onion and anchovy tart (a perfect snack)

¼ cup/50g olive oil

2 pounds/900g onions, thinly sliced

Kosher salt and freshly ground black pepper

All-purpose flour, for dusting

1 disc Whole Wheat Pie Crust (page 281) or The Only Pie Crust (page 280)

1 (2-ounce) tin or 1.5–2-ounce jar of oil-packed anchovy fillets

1 large egg

Flaky sea salt

½ cup parsley (tender leaves and stems), barely chopped

Crushed red pepper flakes

½ lemon

Eat with
Olives. Soft ripe cheese. Warm dates. A hunk of parmesan. Wine. An aperitif spritz.

Do ahead
The onions can be caramelized a week in advance, stored wrapped and refrigerated. The tart can be made a few hours ahead, left at room temperature, not refrigerated. I find refrigerating the anchovies after being baked changes the flavor, and not in a good way.

Isn't it nice that even though this is a dessert book, I can still write a recipe that heavily features anchovies? I guess we really *can* have it all.

Pissaladière is a Provençal dish popular in both France and Italy, often made on a puffy, flatbread dough that reminds me of pizza. It's topped with caramelized onions, lots of anchovies draped across the top in a diamond pattern, and dotted with black olives for good measure. This is a version of that, with the caramelized onions and anchovies baked on pie dough because the only thing I like more than a piece of puffy pizza dough is a piece of crispy pie dough.

This is not really a dinner unto itself, but a beautiful start to one. Concentrated in its salty, savory flavors, it's crispy and jammy, rich and light all at once. It is, as the title has mentioned, the perfect snack.

1 In a large pot, heat the olive oil over medium-low heat. Add all but one good handful of the onions and season with salt and pepper. Cook, stirring occasionally, until the onions are deeply caramelized, totally softened, almost jammy, about 1½ hours (if you notice them getting a little dark, especially in the center of the pot, add a splash of water and reduce your heat). Caramelized onions take an annoyingly long, painstakingly long time. Consider this a meditation in patience. Taste the onions and season with salt and pepper; remove from the heat to cool slightly.

2 Preheat the oven to 425°F. Line a sheet pan with parchment paper.

3 On a lightly floured work surface, roll out the dough to a 14-inch round or a 10 × 14-inch rectangle and transfer to the lined pan. Spread the caramelized onions on top, leaving a 2-inch border all around. Scatter with anchovies (I avoid the traditional crisscross pattern but you do you) and raw onions, then fold the crust up around the edges.

4 Beat the egg with a teaspoon of water, then brush the crust with the egg wash. Sprinkle with flaky salt and bake until the crust is deeply browned and the onions are even more caramelized, 40–45 minutes.

5 Let the tart cool slightly before scattering with parsley, a sprinkle of red pepper flakes, and a squeeze of lemon.

a very tall quiche with zucchini and greens

Makes one deep 9-inch quiche

All-purpose flour, for dusting

1 disc Whole Wheat Pie Crust (page 281) or The Only Pie Crust (page 280)

2 pounds/900g zucchini or other summer squash

1 medium yellow or white onion (about 6 ounces/170g)

Kosher salt and freshly ground black pepper

4 ounces/115g feta cheese, crumbled, or parmesan, grated (about 1 cup)

6 large eggs

1¼ cups/290g heavy cream

2 ounces/60g dark, leafy greens, such as kale or Swiss chard, torn into bite-size pieces (1½ cups)

Zucchini flowers (optional)

Olive oil, for drizzling

Eat with

An open tin of anchovies, a salad of peppery greens and lots of dill with a squeeze of lemon.

Do ahead

The quiche can be baked 2 days ahead, stored loosely wrapped and refrigerated. It can be gently warmed in a 350°F oven if you like, or simply bring it to room temperature before serving.

Once again, I am asking you to use a springform pan. Yes, this quiche can be baked in a deep-dish pie plate (you'll have a bit of custard left over), but it's the springform that'll give you those high sides that scream "drama." While I feel like most quiches rely heavily on the cheese of it all, here it's really the vegetables that are doing most of the work (but of course, there is still cheese). How will two whole pounds of zucchini fit into this quiche? Through the magic of grating, salting, and squeezing, you'll see that zucchini is mostly water and that when all is said and done, you're not left with much zucchini at all. Is zucchini a lie? Seems that way.

Needless to say, that salting and squeezing part is really important to the success of the quiche—too much water left inside the vegetables and you'll be left with a soupy, unsliceable mess. If that step feels annoying, just be grateful (no pun intended) I'm not asking you to cook the zucchini (because if you squeeze it hard enough, there's no need!).

1   Preheat the oven to 375°F.

2   On a lightly floured work surface, roll out the dough to a round about 14 inches in diameter.

3   Transfer the dough round to a 9-inch springform or regular cake pan (line with parchment if using a regular cake pan), pressing into the bottom and up the sides about 2 inches. Using a knife or scissors, trim any overhang.

4   Place a sheet of parchment paper inside the dough and fill it with pie weights or dried beans. Bake until the sides are set and the top is starting to brown, 20–25 minutes. Remove it from the oven and remove the pie weights and parchment. Return the crust to the oven to continue to brown on the bottom, another 10 minutes or so.

Note
In the wintertime, grated raw butternut, kabocha, or acorn squash would also work here; simply substitute the summer squash with same amount of winter squash.

5 Meanwhile, thinly slice a few coins of the zucchini to scatter over the top at the end (just a few pieces; this is purely for decor). Coarsely grate the rest on a box grater (or food processor attachment, if you can find it) along with the onion. Transfer both to a large bowl, season well with salt, toss, and let sit for 10–20 minutes, letting the water come out as the zucchini softens.

6 Once the crust is baked, remove it from the oven and set it aside while you prepare the filling. Using your hands (or a cheesecloth or kitchen towel), squeeze all the water from the zucchini/onion mixture (there will be a lot!). The zucchini/onions should be rather dry by the time you're done with them.

7 In another large bowl, whisk the feta, eggs, and heavy cream together until well blended (some pieces of feta are fine). Add the zucchini/onion mixture and the greens and season well with salt and lots of pepper.

8 Pour the mixture into the prebaked quiche shell and scatter the top with the sliced zucchini coins and zucchini flowers, if available. Drizzle with olive oil and give it another crack of pepper and sprinkle of salt.

9 Bake until the custard is set and no longer jiggles, 40–45 minutes. It should look slightly puffed and browned around the edges, but still pretty blond in the center.

tomato tart

Makes one 9-inch tart

For the crust

6 tablespoons/3 ounces/85g unsalted butter

1 cup/145g all-purpose flour

¼ cup/45g medium-grind cornmeal

1 cup/50g lightly packed finely grated parmesan cheese

1½ teaspoons/6g kosher salt

1 teaspoon/4g sugar

Freshly ground black pepper

For the tart

2 pounds/900g small tomatoes,* thinly sliced

2–4 garlic cloves, very thinly sliced

Kosher salt and freshly ground black pepper

Crushed red pepper flakes

2 tablespoons capers (optional), roughly chopped

2 tablespoons olive oil, plus more for drizzling

1 tablespoon sherry vinegar, red wine vinegar, or white wine vinegar

Herbs/parmesan, for serving

I will not make an exhaustive list of the items in this book that gave me trouble and why they gave me trouble, but this tomato tart gave me more trouble than most things. I knew from moment one that I wanted this to be a quick, throw-together affair. That meant no "salt the tomatoes to draw out the moisture," no crust that needed to be chilled or rolled out, no multistep song and dance when all I wanted was a crisp, cheesy crust with a simple layer of softened, jammy, garlicky tomatoes. How hard could it be?

Well, let's just say I almost gave up more than once, but I'm so glad I didn't. The peppery crust, which I've been told tastes like a Cheez-It or "a refined Dorito," is worth the price of admission alone. An excellent and versatile vehicle for many savory summertime tarts, it's tomatoes that it was truly born to be with, absorbing the juiciness without becoming soggy, staying crunchy and crisp against all odds. A number of things could be added here to your tomatoes, but I like *Goodfellas*-thin slices of raw garlic and capers. Other things include thinly sliced shallot, anchovies (of course), or roughly chopped black olives.

I give the option to make this in a tart pan or a pie plate, but it's really best in the tart pan. Take this as your sign from the universe to finally purchase one. You'll use it all the time, at the very least, for this recipe. Worth it, I promise.

1   **Make the crust:** Preheat the oven to 375°F.

2   In a small pot or skillet, melt the butter over medium-high heat. Whisking occasionally, scrape up the browned bits as they form and continue to cook the butter until it smells like popcorn, 3–5 minutes. Remove from the heat and let cool slightly.

3   In a medium bowl, mix the flour, cornmeal, parmesan, salt, and sugar. Add 2 tablespoons water, plenty of black pepper, and pour the butter over. Using your hands, mix until well combined. The dough will be slightly sticky, but that's okay.

*The beauty of this tart is that it's a great way to use up all your August tomatoes, sure, but it's also shockingly great with out-of-season, available-365-style hothouse vine tomatoes. Whichever you use, try to pick the ones that are on the small side (think golf ball or tangerine), and throw in a few Sungolds, cherry, or grape tomatoes for good measure and textural contrast.

Eat with
A big vinegar-y salad, roasted eggplant, some seasoned ricotta, maybe a side of anchovies.

Do ahead
The tart is best baked and enjoyed the day of, but is still excellent at room temperature the next day.

4 Press the dough into a 9-inch tart pan or regular (not a deep-dish) pie plate, at first making sure the sides are evenly packed, then press a nice, even layer on the bottom. Prick all over with a fork or tip of a knife.

5 Bake until golden brown on the sides and, most important, on the bottom (this is your chance to crisp up the bottom!), 20–25 minutes.

6 Set the crust aside and leave the oven on. (You can bake this shell ahead of time, if you like. Store it wrapped well at room temperature for up to 2 days.)

7 **Assemble the tart:** Arrange the tomato and garlic slices onto the parbaked shell in a nice, even layer, seasoning with pinches of salt, pepper, and red pepper flakes as you go. Top with capers (if using), then drizzle everything with 2 tablespoons olive oil, seasoning again with salt and pepper.

8 Place the tart pan on a sheet pan, return to the oven, and bake until the tomatoes are jammy and starting to brown and caramelize a touch on top, 55–60 minutes.

9 Remove the tart from the oven, splash with the vinegar, give it another drizzle of olive oil and let cool slightly before slicing. Serve with grated/shaved parmesan and some fresh herbs on top, if you'd like.

This tart is main course material, especially when served with a bowlful of creamy cheese, a big herby salad, good anchovies, fried capers, and more tomatoes. It might seem counterintuitive to serve a tomato tart with more tomatoes, but the tomato tart tomatoes are soft, jammy, and caramelized and deserve to be eaten with fresh tomatoes, which are firm and juicy. Tomato season is fleeting. Do not let it pass you by.

creamy cauliflower galette

Makes one 10-inch galette

All-purpose flour, for dusting

1 disc The Only Pie Crust (page 280) or Whole Wheat Pie Crust (page 281)

¾ pound/340g cauliflower, sliced lengthwise through the core into slabs about ¼ inch thick (some of the cauliflower will naturally break away into florets, that's okay)

1 medium leek, thinly sliced

Kosher salt and freshly ground black pepper

1 cup/4 ounces/115g grated white cheddar, Gruyère, or parmesan cheese

2 tablespoons olive oil, plus more for drizzling

½ cup/120g heavy cream

1 large egg

Eat with
A smattering of herbs on top, or next to a big, gorgeous, herby salad with plenty of lemon, and maybe more cheese on the side.

Do ahead
This galette can be baked 2 days ahead and stored loosely wrapped at room temperature. It can be refrigerated up to 5 days, and is great cold, but you can also rewarm it in a 350°F oven.

Cauliflower is an ideal candidate for a savory galette. It's low in moisture, roasting to an evenly golden brown in sync with the crunchy, buttery crust. It never becomes soggy, is great at room temperature, and can handle a healthy amount of cheese without disappearing into the background. This is the galette you make when you need something substantial and comforting, don't feel like eating meat, and have had too much pasta or are—god forbid—sick of beans. While this certainly could be served as your full dinner, I also like the idea of slicing it thin and enjoying it as a predinner snack, next to a little dish of olives and some hard, salty cheese.

I have it on good authority (because I did it) that this also works with wedges of cabbage (about 1 inch thick) in place of cauliflower—highly recommend.

1 Preheat the oven to 375°F.

2 On a lightly floured work surface, roll the dough out to a round about 14 inches in diameter, give or take. Transfer the dough round to a piece of parchment paper on a sheet pan.

3 Leaving a 2-inch border all around, scatter the sliced cauliflower and leeks over the dough, seasoning with pinches of salt and pepper throughout. Scatter with the cheese, drizzle with the olive oil, and fold up the edges onto each other.

4 Pour the heavy cream over the vegetables and cheese, followed by another little drizzle of olive oil. Beat the egg with a teaspoon or so of water, then brush the egg wash all over the crust. Sprinkle with some black pepper.

5 Bake, rotating the pan front to back once halfway through (or twice, if you know your oven is especially uneven), until the crust of the galette is deeply golden brown (think the color of graham crackers), the cauliflower is totally tender, and the top looks gloriously roasted, 55–65 minutes.

6 Let cool slightly before slicing and eating.

many mushrooms pot pie

Makes one 9-inch pot pie

2 discs* The Only Pie Crust (page 280)

⅓ cup/70g olive oil

1½ pounds/680g mixed mushrooms, such as maitake, oyster, cremini, or button, torn or cut into bite-size pieces

Kosher salt and freshly ground black pepper

4 garlic cloves, thinly sliced

1 medium onion, thinly sliced

2 tablespoons/1 ounce/30g unsalted butter

3 tablespoons fresh thyme, oregano, or marjoram leaves

¼ cup/35g all-purpose flour

2½ cups vegetable broth, chicken broth, or water**

½ cup/120g heavy cream

1 cup parsley, tender leaves and stems, finely chopped

1 large egg

Flaky sea salt

* This can be more a traditional pot pie with one crust, if you like. See the directions for how to accomplish this.

** If using water, consider adding a generous splash or two of soy sauce to season it a bit.

This is probably the best-tasting thing in the whole book—we aren't supposed to say things like that, and I also know that I am likely to change my mind fifty-three times between now and when this book is published. But today, on this gray wintry day, I am imagining a creamy mushroom filling made of many mushrooms (as advertised), baked between two pieces of flaky, perfectly salty, almost-too-buttery pie crust. I am thinking of how creamy the filling is, how rich and meaty it tastes without any meat at all, and how despite my obsession with chicken pot pie, this mushroom pot pie is admittedly better. I love this mushroom pot pie for dinner alongside a bitter chicory salad, for a late lunch with orange wine, for eating in front of the TV with no plates, just forks.

This could be made in the more traditional pot-pie style of one crust with the filling below, but I really love baking it as a "regular" pie, with a crust above and below. While this isn't necessarily designed to be a perfectly sliceable pie, it is possible that with enough patience, this pie can be sliced. For the rest of us with no patience, you can serve it by scooping with a large serving spoon.

1　Preheat the oven to 400°F. Line a sheet pan with parchment paper.

2　On a lightly floured work surface, roll both discs of dough out to rounds 12–14 inches in diameter. Lay one into a 9-inch pie plate (ideally a glass one) and gently drape the second round of dough over the first. Refrigerate while you prepare the filling. (If you are just using one crust, roll it out and refrigerate it flat on a baking sheet while you make the filling.)

3　In a large skillet, heat the olive oil over medium-high heat. Add half the mushrooms and season with kosher salt and pepper. Cook, stirring occasionally, until the mushrooms shrink in size and begin to brown, 5–8 minutes. Add the remaining mushrooms, season with salt and pepper, and continue to cook until all the mushrooms are about the same size and tenderness, on their way to golden brown, another 8–10 minutes.

4   Add the garlic and onion and continue cooking until the mushrooms and onions are deeply browned, frizzled, and caramelized at the edges (they should still be tender in the center), another 10–15 minutes.

5   Reduce the heat to medium and add the butter and thyme, letting the butter melt around the mushrooms. Add the flour and stir to coat the mushrooms. Cook until the flour starts to toast in the skillet (it should smell like browning butter or toast), 2–3 minutes. Slowly add the broth, stirring to combine (it'll be quite thick at first, but will loosen up). Add the heavy cream and simmer until the mixture is thick enough to coat the back of a spoon—not soupy, but not a paste, about 5 minutes. Add the parsley, season with kosher salt and pepper, and remove from the heat.

6   Remove the pie plate from the fridge and set it on the lined sheet pan. Set the second round of dough aside. Fill the pie plate with the mushroom mixture (it should come just up to the top of the pie plate). Lay the reserved dough round on top. Using the tines of a fork, press the top and bottom crusts together, sealing the mushroom mixture inside. Using a small knife or scissors, trim the excess dough so that there's not much overhang. (If you are just using one crust, simply fill a 9-inch pie plate or an 8- or 9-inch cast-iron skillet with the prepared mushroom mixture and top with the round of dough. Trim overhang and crimp the dough.)

7   Mix the egg with a teaspoon of water and brush the top of the crust with the egg wash. Sprinkle with flaky salt and more black pepper. Make a few incisions or slits in the top of the crust (more toward the center than the sides).

8   Bake the pie until the crust is deeply golden brown all over, on the top and underneath (baking enough underneath is important to avoid a soggy bottom—this is where a glass pie plate comes in handy), 1 hour 10 minutes to 1 hour 20 minutes.

9   Let cool slightly before eating.

no plates

just forks

cakes

If I'm being honest, I was for many years not really a cake person. They always sort of seemed like decor, a thing you'd present when you had to celebrate something without much regard for how it actually tasted. But over time, I decided I loved different types of cakes—cakes with sticky bottoms, cakes made with mostly cheese, cakes that were so fluffy and light they could and certainly should be eaten for breakfast. None of the cakes in this chapter are going to win any showstopper or architectural awards—that's not really my speed—but they are pleasantly simple, extremely delicious, and shockingly easy to make.

Above all other desserts, I believe that cakes should be as unfussy as humanly possible, requiring little more than a bowl or two, a spatula or whisk, and of course, a cake pan (although we could work around that if needed). They should be baked to an irresistibly golden brown and crack pleasantly around the edges. They should welcome fruit with open arms (baked inside or served alongside) or be right at home with nothing but a cup of strong tea. They are meant for a party, to be gifted, and also only for yourself. Frosted or not, candles are always optional, and in lieu of slicing, sometimes it just feels right to break off a piece of cake with your hands. Baker or person-who-doesn't-bake, these cakes are for everyone—yes, even you.

old-fashioned strawberry cake

Makes one 9-inch cake

Cooking spray

2 cups/290g all-purpose flour

2 teaspoons/8g baking powder

¾ teaspoon/3g kosher salt

1 stick/4 ounces/115g unsalted butter, at room temperature

⅓ cup/70g granulated sugar

⅓ cup/75g light brown sugar

1 teaspoon vanilla extract

2 large eggs

¾ cup/180g buttermilk

10 ounces/295g strawberries, hulled and sliced ¼ inch thick (or halved blackberries, blueberries, pitted sweet cherries, sliced peaches, or figs)

3 tablespoons demerara sugar (you can use granulated sugar in a pinch)

Eat with
Your hands!

Do ahead
This cake can be baked 3 days ahead, tightly wrapped with plastic wrap, and stored at room temperature.

As you may have noticed, there is no deep-frying in this book. Not because I don't enjoy the occasional donut, cruller, churro, or other deep-fried delight, but because: No, I will not be doing that. I will not heat up a large pot of oil and drop in the batter and fry, hoping I have not undercooked the insides or overly fried the outsides, then have to deal with the hot oil—even typing that feels exhausting. Not in my home, anyway.

But the taste. The taste of a cake donut haunts me. Its vaguely vanilla flavor, deeply golden exterior, crumbly-yet-compact interior is hard to get without a fryer. Yet somehow this cake comes extremely close.

1   Preheat the oven to 350°F. Spray the bottom of a 9-inch cake pan with cooking spray and line with parchment paper (either cut to fit the bottom, or leaving some hanging over the edges for easy removal).

2   In a medium bowl, whisk the flour, baking powder, and salt together.

3   In a stand mixer fitted with the paddle (or in a large bowl with an electric hand mixer), beat the butter, granulated sugar, brown sugar, and vanilla together on medium-high, periodically scraping down the sides of the bowl to make sure everything incorporates, until the mixture is pale, light, fluffy, and creamy, about 5 minutes.

4   Add the eggs, one at a time, beating to blend after each addition. (This is a good time to scrape down the sides again.)

5   Reduce the mixer speed to low and carefully add half the flour mixture, followed by half the buttermilk. Repeat with the remaining flour mixture and buttermilk, beating just until no large lumps remain.

6   Using a spatula, gently fold in half the strawberries and transfer the batter to the prepared cake pan. Scatter with the remaining strawberries and sprinkle with demerara sugar. Bake until the cake is puffed, deeply golden brown, and pulling away at the sides, 45–50 minutes. (It should spring back slightly when pressed in the center and appear fully baked where the strawberries meet the cake.)

7   Let the cake cool completely before eating.

anytime shortcake

Serves 6–8, depending

1½ cups/220g all-purpose flour, plus more for dusting

¼ cup/40g yellow cornmeal

2 tablespoons/25g granulated sugar, plus more for sprinkling

2 tablespoons/25g light brown sugar

1 tablespoon/12g baking powder

¾ teaspoon/3g kosher salt

1 stick/4 ounces/115g cold unsalted butter, cut into 1-inch pieces

½ cup/110g heavy cream, plus more for brushing

Flaky sea salt, for sprinkling

Eat with
If you're going a simple shortcake route rather than any of the "choose your own adventure" options listed, I would personally eat these shortcakes with a bit of honey butter or clotted cream.

Do ahead
Shortcakes, as is, are best the day they are baked. The dough can be made a day ahead, stored wrapped in the refrigerator.

A good shortcake recipe is great to have in your back pocket for when you're in the mood for a little sweet cake-y something (without like, you know, baking a whole cake). Less flaky and slightly sweeter than a biscuit, shortcake occupies a similar space in that it's good with everything, able to be baked in myriad ways, in whatever shape you please, without the need for any special equipment. It's a true chameleon, and greater than the sum of its parts.

Bake it into one large shortcake on a sheet pan and break up into pieces to layer it in an obnoxiously large bowl with fresh fruit and something creamy for a casual trifle (page 95). Or punch out smaller rounds and bake them atop fruit, sugar, and cornstarch for what counts as a cobbler to at least half of the people reading this (page 271). Or maybe just cut fat little squares from the dough, bake, and eat as is with a bit of whipped cream or softened honey butter. Whatever you do, don't forget to brush the top with a little extra cream (milk, buttermilk, melted butter, or an egg wash also work) and sprinkle with sugar (regular, brown, demerara) before baking: It's what gives the top that appealing caramelized, come-hither crackle.

1   Preheat the oven to 425°F.

2   In a large bowl, combine the flour, cornmeal, granulated sugar, brown sugar, baking powder, and salt. Using your hands, rub the butter into the flour mixture until no large chunks remain. Add the cream and mix with your hands just until blended. Turn the dough out onto a lightly floured work surface and knead the dough just until it's no longer super sticky, about 2 minutes.

3   Cut and bake the dough depending on your intended application and the shortcake's final destination. Read on for some suggestions.

For anytime shortcakes

1 Using your hands, pat the dough into a round about 1½ inches thick.

2 Either cut into 8 even wedges (like a scone) or use a cookie cutter (or mason jar) to punch out rounds of whatever size you prefer. Place them on a parchment-lined sheet pan, brush with cream, and sprinkle with sugar.

3 Bake, rotating the pan front to back once, until the shortcakes are golden brown at the edges and tops feel a bit firm and baked through when lightly pressed, 10–12 minutes. Remove from the oven and sprinkle the top with flaky sea salt.

For casual trifle

1 Place the dough on a parchment-lined sheet pan.

2 Using your hands, pat the dough down to about 1 inch thick—it doesn't matter what shape here, just make sure it's evenly thick, especially at the edges.

3 Brush with cream, sprinkle with sugar, and bake, rotating the pan front to back once or so until the shortcake is puffed and golden, and the top feels a bit firm and baked through when lightly pressed, 20–25 minutes.

4 Continue with the instructions in Naked Peaches on page 228.

For a breakfast cobbler

1 Replace all of the cornmeal and ¼ cup/36g flour with quick-cooking oats. For even better flavor, toast the oats in a small skillet before using.

2 On a lightly floured work surface, knead the dough just until it's no longer super-sticky. Pat it out so it's about 1½ inches thick. (The shape here doesn't matter; you'll be cutting out rounds.)

3 Using a 2-inch round cutter, or something approximately that size (water glasses and mason jars also work), punch out as many shortcakes as you can. Gently gather and re-pat the scraps and repeat until all the dough is used. You should have enough dough for 8–10 shortcakes. Continue with the recipe on page 271.

Either slice the cake into elegant shapes to serve with tea, or use your hands to break it up in irregular clusters that resemble icebergs. The craggy edges are ideal for absorbing the juiciness of naked peaches (page 228) or freshly cut strawberries and the creaminess of whipped cream or vanilla pudding (page 158).

There are a lot of reasons to attempt a classic dessert, but historically, I have always found it to be emotionally easier to double-down on making something same-but-different. Otherwise, people get too attached to something they think they want, and the expectations simply get too high. When you make a recipe for something that's already iconic and call it "the one," "the only," "the best," or "the ultimate," you're setting a lot of people up to be skeptical or, worse, disappointed. Even sometimes just saying "This is a carrot cake recipe" will knock someone's universe askew if it's not done to the exact specifications as the one they had growing up, from that one bakery that always piped carrots on top in orange frosting.

I use carrot cake as a premier example of this because the range is so drastic (not unlike a chocolate chip cookie, which, you know, I'm not going there). When it comes to carrot cakes, there are fluffy ones, dense ones, frosted ones, ones with raisins or walnuts, layered ones, ones baked in loaf pans and sliced, and ones baked in sheet pans and frosted. Some are heavily spiced, some have nary a whisper of cinnamon. This is a gentle way of saying there's no way any one recipe will be everybody's favorite, and I could never say that something is The One or The Only unless I truly believed there was no better way (see: The Only Pie Crust, page 280). But on the following pages, I have written what I think is one very good recipe for a carrot cake that is, by any account, a little untraditional but still undeniably a carrot cake. Please know that I have no problem with what your idea of a perfect carrot cake is, regardless of what you have (or don't have) in it, but I am ready to defend within an inch of my life my decisions of what makes this one very good. After all, recipes don't just "happen"; they must be considered and full of purpose.

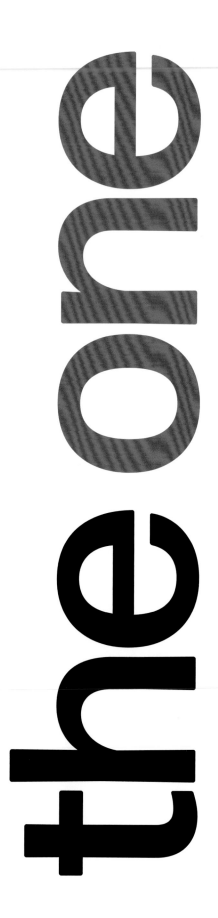

the one

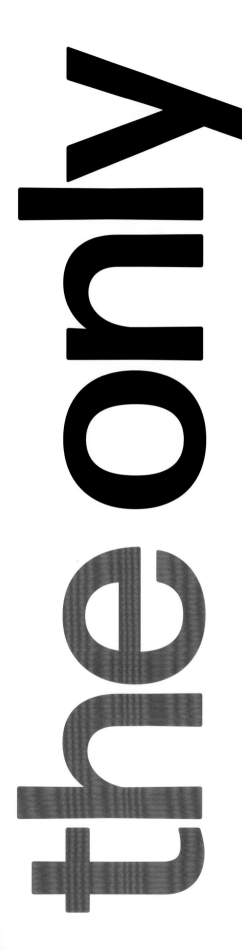

the only

First of all, no raisins in my carrot cake. No raisins in this whole book because, sorry, they just aren't for me. As a consolation, there are dates, which I find to be infinitely more pleasant in a carrot cake. They echo the brown sugar, while contributing their own caramel-like flavor with a sticky quality that some might read as "moistness." Also, an important thing to mention about dates is that a date is not a raisin.

Second, no walnuts. No nuts in this cake at all, actually. I love a crunchy walnut as much as the next person, which is exactly why I will not put it into a cake batter to become a soggy, weaker version of its former self. There are no walnuts in this cake because I respect walnuts too much. If you just simply MUST have a walnut in your carrot cake, then please do not let me stop you, but good luck forgetting the phrase "soggy walnut."

Third, this carrot cake is on the denser side, as it is not a cake with a suggestion of carrot; it is a cake made mostly of carrots. That's not to say it doesn't still have a delicate, airy crumb—it does. But it's also got this slightly sticky-toffee-pudding-ish thing happening (another reason dates are good) that's got a texture not unlike A Better Banana Bread (page 272), which incidentally is also walnut-free.

Fourth, it's not really meant to be baked and layered but, rather, more simply baked in its little round and enjoyed on its own or with a thin smear of frosting. Neither the cake nor the frosting requires a mixer.

Fifth, no, it doesn't have to be refrigerated, but per its title (again, named with intention), refrigerating it will give you the advertised slice of cold carrot cake, one of the most delightful textures and flavors in this whole world.

cold carrot cake

For the cake

Cooking spray

1¼ cups/180g all-purpose flour

1½ teaspoons/3g ground cinnamon

1 teaspoon/6g baking soda

1 teaspoon/4g kosher salt

1 teaspoon/4g baking powder

½ teaspoon/1g ground turmeric, cardamom, or ginger (optional)

3 large eggs

¾ cup/155g light brown sugar

⅔ cup/145g sour cream or Greek yogurt

1 pound/455g carrots, peeled and grated

10–12 Medjool dates (8 ounces/225g), pitted and chopped

4 tablespoons/2 ounces/56g unsalted butter, melted

¼ cup/50g vegetable or olive oil

Eat with
A quiche on a cute picnic.

Do ahead
Carrot cake can be baked 2 days ahead, tightly wrapped in plastic, and refrigerated. Frosted, it can be loosely covered and refrigerated for up to 2 days.

This carrot cake, sans raisins and nuts (!!) is, to me, perfect. If you can believe it, it doesn't really need frosting, although I do understand the sentimental attachment. While the salty vanilla frosting (page 293) would be excellent, I know what you want is cream cheese frosting, preferably one that doesn't require a mixer (just like this cake).

For quick cream cheese frosting, combine 8 ounces/225g of softened cream cheese, ½ cup/60g powdered sugar, and a good pinch of kosher salt together in a medium bowl. Use a fork to combine everything (this is why the cream cheese needs to be at room temperature) until smooth, like softened butter. Spread onto the cake and sprinkle with chopped, toasted nuts if you like.

1   Preheat the oven to 350°F. Line a 9-inch cake pan with a round of parchment paper and spray with cooking spray.

2   In a large bowl, whisk together the flour, cinnamon, baking soda, salt, baking powder, and turmeric (if using).

3   In another large bowl, whisk the eggs, brown sugar, and sour cream together until well blended. Add the carrots and dates and, using a spatula or wooden spoon, mix until all the bits are evenly dispersed. Pour the wet ingredients into the dry ingredients and use a spatula to mix until just combined. Add the melted butter along with the oil and stop mixing as soon as you've got a nice, even batter.

4   Pour the batter into the prepared cake pan and bake until the top is puffed and golden and the sides pull away from the pan, 40–45 minutes.

5   This cake can be eaten now, or, for what I think is the optimal carrot cake experience, refrigerate it until completely chilled before slicing.

bonnie's pineapple upside-down cake

Makes one 9- or 10-inch cake

For the topping
(which is actually the bottom)

Cooking spray or softened butter, for the pan

½ cup/105g light brown sugar

About ½ pineapple, peeled, cored, and sliced about ½ inch thick*

4–6 maraschino cherries, stemmed

2 tablespoons dark rum or brandy (optional)

*When slicing the pineapple and arranging it in the cake pan, perhaps there's space for pineapple that doesn't quite fit a perfect ring. That's okay! Cut the rings in half, make the pineapple work for you, not the other way around. Or maybe you find yourself with a few extra slices, or a pile of scraps. This is great! You can either finely chop about 1 cup of the pineapple and fold it into the cake batter, freeze the scraps for smoothies, or simply eat them as a snack.

Pineapple upside-down cake is an icon. It's your aunt's favorite poolside caftan, a pair of oversize gold-rimmed sunglasses, a hat you bought on vacation and thought "I can pull this off, right?" It's kitsch, it's camp, it's ironic, it's fun, and it's undeniably delicious. It's all-occasion appropriate, seasonally agnostic, and somehow, always just the thing.

Despite this recipe's title, we never did find Grandma Bonnie's original pineapple upside-down cake recipe, but my stepmom is pretty sure it was just a yellow boxed cake mix with booze added in (the rum adds a lot, and obviously I kept it). While it's hard to improve upon the flavor, texture, and general perfection of a yellow cake from a box, this version comes close, I promise (if you wanted to use cake from a box, I would be the last person to stop you).

If pineapple isn't for you, or you can't find one that's even close to ripe (pineapples don't ripen after they're picked, so if it's not ripe at the store, it won't ripen on your counter), this cake is great for any fruit that becomes tender but not mushy when baked: apples, pears, nectarines, peaches, apricots, plums, and cherries. Blackberries might work if you don't mind the texture of their tiny, toothsome core, but I feel like raspberries would be too seedy, blueberries too juicy, strawberries too mushy.

1 **Make the topping:** Preheat the oven to 350°F. Spray a 9- or 10-inch cake pan with cooking spray or grease with butter. (The general opulent vibe of pineapple upside-down cake really deserves a 10-inch cake pan—although it will work in a 9- or 8-inch pan; just know in the case of the 9-inch the cake will be thicker than intended, and with the 8-inch, you'll have a bit of leftover batter.) Sprinkle the brown sugar on the bottom of the cake pan (it will look like a lot of sugar, and it is, but it's not too much, I promise).

2 Mosaic the pineapple on the bottom of the cake pan, cutting pieces to fit the edges as needed. Decorate how you please with your cherries— I'm a fan of the classic one cherry in the center of each ring of pineapple. Isn't that sweet? I think so. Drizzle rum over the pineapple, if using.

2 cups/290g all-purpose or
cake flour

1½ teaspoons/6g baking powder

1 teaspoon/4g kosher salt

¾ teaspoon/5g baking soda

¾ cup/180g buttermilk

½ cup/105g vegetable oil

1 tablespoon/15g dark rum or
brandy (optional)

1 teaspoon/5g vanilla extract

6 tablespoons/3 ounces/85g
unsalted butter, cut into 1-inch
pieces, at room temperature

1 cup/220g granulated sugar

½ cup/85g packed light brown
sugar

3 large eggs

2 large egg yolks

Eat with
This cake needs nothing other
than sunshine and a good attitude.

Do ahead
The cake can be baked and
unmolded 2 days ahead of time,
tightly wrapped with plastic wrap,
and stored at room temperature.

3 **Make the batter:** In a large bowl, whisk the flour, baking powder, salt, and baking soda together. In a medium bowl or a measuring cup, combine the buttermilk, vegetable oil, rum (if using), and the vanilla.

4 In a stand mixer fitted with the paddle (or in a large bowl with an electric hand mixer), combine the butter, granulated sugar, and brown sugar and beat everything together on high speed until it's super light and fluffy, about 4 minutes. Add the whole eggs and egg yolks one at a time, incorporating each one before adding the next. Beat the batter until it's almost doubled in volume and very light and fluffy, about 5 minutes. (Don't forget to scrape down the sides of the bowl periodically.)

5 With the mixer on low, gently beat in one-third of the flour mixture. Before it's fully combined, add half of the buttermilk mixture. Repeat with another one-third of the flour and the remaining buttermilk, and end with the remaining flour, beating until everything is well blended and no lumps remain.

6 Pour the cake batter over the prepared pineapple and smooth the top. Bake until the cake is golden brown, pulling away from the sides of the pan, and the top springs back ever so slightly when pressed, 40–45 minutes (if your pineapple is ripe, you should also notice quite a bit of bubbling up of the sugar and juices on the sides of the pan— this is a good sign!).

7 Remove the cake from the oven and let it cool for 5–10 minutes before inverting it onto a large plate or platter (whatever it is, just make sure it's wider than the cake pan), using a butter knife or offset spatula to coax it from the pan if needed.

A cake that will inspire you to immediately text your favorite person and demand they make it.

how to

how to core and slice pineapple

To cut pineapple for a pineapple upside-down cake (or to stick to the exterior of a ham, I suppose), you'll want to first remove the prickly skin and the fibrous core, leaving a hollowed-out cylinder of tropical fruit. I find the best way to do this is in a few easy steps:

1   Use a serrated knife, if available, to remove both the bottom and top of the pineapple (this creates an even, secure place for the pineapple to stand up without wobbling). Set the top aside, thinking you might use it to decorate a fruit plate later or make your pet wear it as a hat, but end up doing none of that and throwing it away.

2   With the pineapple standing up vertically, start at the top and peel the skin with a knife down to the bright yellow flesh, working in about 1½-inch-wide increments. As you do this, you might see some "eyes" of the pineapple staring back at you. Do not be alarmed, they cannot see you. Remove them with a swift shave of your knife, attempting to leave as much fruit behind as possible.

3   Assuming you don't have a pineapple corer (but if you do, use it!), place the skinned pineapple lying horizontally on its side. Slice the pineapple crosswise into three even sections. Flip the sections so they are standing vertically on the cutting board, then insert a small paring knife where the core meets the fruit and trace the circle, going a bit deeper each time, until you've successfully come out the other side. It won't be perfect, but you're not a machine so that's okay. Eventually, the core should be easily pushed out with your fingertips. Do not attempt to eat the core, even though you think it might be delicious (it is not).

4   For the upside-down cake (or any application where you want sliced pineapple rings), slice the hollowed-out hunks of pineapple crosswise into rings ¼–½ inch thick. Too thick and they'll never soften in the cake, too thin and they won't give up enough juices to make the whole thing worth your while.

festive yellow sheet cake

Makes one 13 × 18-inch sheet cake or three 9-inch cake layers

Cooking spray or softened butter, for the pan

3¼ cups/470g cake or all-purpose flour

2 teaspoons/8g baking powder

1 teaspoon/6g baking soda

1½ teaspoons/6g kosher salt

1 cup/240g buttermilk

⅔ cup/138g vegetable oil

2 teaspoons/10g vanilla extract

1 stick/4 ounces/115g unsalted butter, cut into 1-inch pieces, at room temperature

1 ¾ cups/385g granulated sugar

½ cup/100g packed light brown sugar

4 large eggs

2 large egg yolks

1½ cups/335g chocolate chips (optional)

Tangy Chocolate Frosting (page 292) or Salty Vanilla Frosting (page 293)

Sometimes a recipe likes to be revisited, updated, refreshed—such is the case with this yellow cake. It's effectively a version of my Celebration Cake that I've been making for years and has been published in at least three different places, but this one has been reworked and redone to thrive in a standard half-sheet pan. Ideal for anyone who is intimidated by the idea of assembling a layer cake, or simply doesn't own cake pans (but, not for nothing, it also bakes beautifully in three 9-inch cake pans), it's still celebratory all the same—festive, even. To me, this classic yellow cake, impossibly golden from eggs, buttermilk, and light brown sugar, will always and forever be my favorite.

As for the frosting, it's really up to you. Despite my loyalty to vanilla, this cake is undeniably perfect with tangy chocolate frosting. Slathered while almost still too warm, the combo reminds me of a very good chocolate chip cookie (if you want to take that fantasy to another level, yes, you can add chocolate chips to the cake batter before baking).

1   Preheat the oven to 350°F. Spray a half-sheet pan (13 × 18 inches) with cooking spray and line with parchment paper. (Alternatively, spray three 9-inch cake pans with cooking spray and line with rounds of parchment paper.)

2   In a large bowl, whisk the flour, baking powder, baking soda, and salt together. In a medium bowl or a measuring cup, combine the buttermilk, vegetable oil, and vanilla.

3   In a stand mixer fitted with the paddle (or in a large bowl with a hand mixer), beat the butter, granulated sugar, and brown sugar on high speed until it's super light and fluffy, about 4 minutes. Add the whole eggs and egg yolks one at a time, incorporating each one before adding the next. Beat the mixture until it's almost doubled in volume and very light and fluffy, about 5 minutes. (Don't forget to scrape down the sides of the bowl periodically.)

Do ahead
Wrapped tightly in plastic wrap,
the cake can last 2 days stored
at room temperature, 5 days in
the fridge, or up to 1 month in the
freezer (I'd wrap it once more in
aluminum foil if freezing).

4 With the mixer on low, gently beat in one-third of the flour mixture. Before it's fully combined, add half of the buttermilk mixture. Repeat with another one-third of the flour and the remaining buttermilk, and end with the remaining flour, until everything is well blended and no lumps remain. Fold in the chocolate chips, if using.

5 Pour the batter into the prepared sheet pan (or divide the batter among the three cake pans) and bake, rotating the pan(s) front to back once, until the cake is baked through, which means golden brown at the edges, slightly more pale golden brown on top, and springing back ever so slightly when lightly pressed on top, 40–45 minutes (30–35 minutes for individual cakes).

6 **To frost either the yellow or chocolate sheet cakes (page 112):**
Remove the cake(s) from the oven and let cool (preferably on a wire rack). To remove, use an offset spatula or butter knife to run around the edges of the pan, making sure no cake sticks to the pan. Lay a large piece of parchment paper onto the counter and invert the cake.

7 **To frost:** You can frost the entire sheet pan cake and cut little squares, that's nice. Or you can cut the whole sheet pan in half and stack the two halves, with frosting between the layers, that's nice, too! Or, you can cut the cake into halves or quarters and freeze some for another time before you frost. There are truly no limits here. If you've made the round cakes and want to make a layer cake, spoon ½–⅓ cup frosting between the layers. Leave the outside nude and exposed, or frost the sides and top, too.

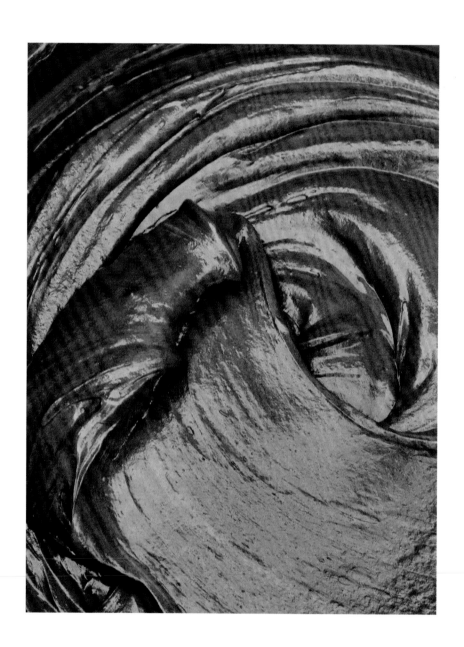

all-purpose chocolate sheet cake

Makes one 13 × 18-inch sheet cake or three 9-inch cake layers

Cooking spray, for the pan

2½ cups/360g all-purpose flour

1 cup/115g unsweetened cocoa powder*

2 teaspoons/8g baking powder

1 teaspoon/6g baking soda

2 teaspoons/8g kosher salt

1¼ cups/275g granulated sugar

1 cup/200g light brown sugar

1½ teaspoons/7g vanilla extract

3 large eggs

1½ cups/330g buttermilk

¾ cup/155g vegetable oil

1 cup/220g sour cream

* Cocoa powder absorbs liquid differently than plain flour, so there's an above-average amount of liquid and fat in this recipe to compensate for the amount needed to give you that promised chocolaty flavor. You may think the batter looks a bit loose when it goes into the oven, but trust, it's going to turn out great.

Do ahead
Wrapped tightly in plastic wrap, the cake can last 3 days stored at room temperature, 5 days in the fridge, or up to 1 month in the freezer (I'd wrap it once more in aluminum foil if freezing).

There are lots of great things about this chocolate sheet cake, not least of all, we are talking about a whole sheet of CAKE, hello! But the two most important things are that (1) It doesn't require a mixer of any sort, which is great because who has the time, and (2) It's got a real, honest-to-god chocolate flavor without the inclusion of any solid chocolate (which in my opinion, can make for a dry cake). It's a truly and genuinely easy cake that doesn't sacrifice any sort of structural integrity, baking up tall and proud, fluffy and tender in all the right places, not unlike a boxed mix (if you're looking for a denser, chocolaty CHOCOLATE number, check out the pound cake on page 133).

While this cake can be treated and dressed with a number of accoutrements, it's tough to beat the two premier examples given in this book. When paired with Salty Vanilla Frosting (page 293), it evokes "Ding-Dong," the Hostess cake I still fantasize about on a regular basis. When used as the base for ice cream cake, specifically with mint and chip ice cream (see Mint and Chip Ice Cream Cake, page 204), it's transformed into what is arguably the best dessert on the planet (sure, I've said this before—I'll say it again!).

1 Preheat the oven to 350°F. Spray a standard half-sheet pan (13 × 18 inches) with cooking spray and line with parchment paper. (Alternatively, spray three 9-inch cake pans with cooking spray and line with rounds of parchment paper.)

2 In a medium bowl, whisk together the flour, cocoa powder, baking powder, baking soda, and salt.

3 In a large bowl, whisk the granulated sugar, brown sugar, vanilla, eggs, buttermilk, vegetable oil, and sour cream until combined. Slowly whisk in the flour mixture.

4 Pour the batter into the prepared sheet pan (or cake pans) and bake until the cake is puffed, springing back and pulling away from the sides of the pan, 30–35 minutes (closer to 20–25 minutes for the individual cakes).

5 Let cool completely before frosting or using to make an ice cream cake.

semolina cake with lemon and fennel

Makes one 9-inch cake

Cooking spray, softened/melted butter, or neutral oil, for the pan

1¼ cups/250g sugar

2 tablespoons finely grated lemon zest

1 teaspoon/2g fennel seeds, crushed or finely chopped

1 cup/230g whole-milk yogurt (not Greek)

2 large eggs

1 cup/145g all-purpose flour

½ cup/85g semolina flour

1 tablespoon/12g baking powder

1 teaspoon/4g kosher salt

⅓ cup/70g olive, grapeseed, or canola oil

Eat with
A cup of tea, a cup of coffee, a cup of coffee followed by a cup of tea.

Do ahead
The cake can be baked 3 days ahead of time, tightly wrapped in plastic wrap, and stored at room temperature.

My friend Tom, who tested some of the recipes in this book, texted me after baking this cake: "Alison, this cake! The lemon! The fennel! It's just so elegant." I told him that just because we are friends, he was not allowed to lie to me to feed my ego, but don't worry—he would never do that. I originally thought of this cake as a sort of humble snacking cake, something to nibble alongside a 2 p.m. coffee or tea without much thought. But he's right. It *is* elegant.

The fennel (subtle but necessary) and the lemon (present enough to pique your interest but not so much that I'd call it a "lemon cake") show up to support and enhance the semolina rather than upstage it. The semolina, more delicate than cornmeal both in flavor and texture, gives so much more tender crumb than an all-flour cake is capable of. It really is pure elegance, all the way.

1   Preheat the oven to 375°F. Lightly grease a 9-inch cake pan with cooking spray, butter, or oil and line with a round of parchment.

2   In a medium bowl and using your hands, mix the sugar, lemon zest, and fennel seeds together until the texture resembles wet sand. Whisk in the yogurt and eggs.

3   In a large bowl, whisk together the flour, semolina, baking powder, and salt. Whisk in the yogurt mixture and oil until blended.

4   Pour the batter into the prepared cake pan and bake until the cake is golden brown on top and along the edges (it might look freckled/slightly spotted, which is good!) and the cake is pulling away from the sides of the pan, 30–35 minutes.

5   Let cool slightly before turning out onto a wire rack to cool completely.

This cake is the cake that started it all.

the near impossibility and radical joy of an almost one-bowl cake

The Raspberry Ricotta Cake on the next page is the cake that started it all—"it all" being the beginning of my love affair with simple one-bowl cakes (sure, technically there are two bowls, but only one for the batter! You get the idea). I originally published the following recipe for a raspberry ricotta cake in 2015, which, by today's calendar, means I'm eighty-nine years old. At the time of inception, I was a few years out of a career in "fine-dining" restaurants, where the desserts I used to make not only required a mixer, they required Pacojets and lamination machines, silicone molds, and Silpats.

In this new life as a home cook magazine editor who wrote recipes for the home cook, I wanted cake, but I didn't want to sift, or use a mixer, or even pick up an offset spatula. I wanted a bowl and a whisk and a cake pan. Looking back, the impulse to make such a bare-bones cake was so clearly a rebellion against the years of fussiness, dirty dishes, and multiple steps.

At first, even I was skeptical of this recipe working. How could a cake that came together in one bowl ever compete with one that started with proper creaming of butter and sugar, emulsified eggs, delicately added sifted flour (just kidding, I never sifted)? On the other hand, there was just so. much. ricotta.

I made quite a few versions, some custardy and unsliceable, some rubbery and inedible. When I finally "got it," I surprised even myself with just how good it was. No mixer? Frozen fruit? I feel like everyone who tries it is equally surprised in the best way possible.

This cake has given birth to many other cakes throughout the years. Some heavy on the citrus, some laced with coconut or cocoa powder. Some with fresh fruit, others swirled with jam (like the variation mentioned in the headnote of this recipe). Every time, it produces something that's nothing short of spectacular. Perhaps my favorite example of just how magical baking really is.

raspberry ricotta cake

Makes one 9-inch cake

Cooking spray

1½ cups/220g all-purpose flour

1 tablespoon/12g baking powder

1 teaspoon/4g kosher salt

1½ cups/365g ricotta cheese

1¼ cups/275g sugar

Grated zest of 1 lemon, lime, grapefruit, or orange (optional)

3 large eggs

½ teaspoon/2g vanilla extract

1 stick/4 ounces/115g unsalted butter, melted

12–16 ounces/340g–450g raspberries or blackberries, fresh or frozen

Eat with
A bowl of ricotta (sweetened or unsweetened) on the side (you know you want to).

Do ahead
This cake can be baked 3 days ahead, tightly wrapped in plastic, and stored at room temperature.

This cake is on the less-sweet side, precisely my intention. But if you're craving something a bit stickier, a bit sweeter, know that this versatile batter can be baked with 1 cup of jam or marmalade (any of your choice, but I really recommend the chunkier "oven jam" as described on page 239) swirled in in lieu of the unsweetened berries. The result will be a little sweeter and a bit more subtle in its delivery of the fruit, thanks to the even distribution, but still very delicious and extremely snackable.

1 Preheat the oven to 350°F. Spray a 9-inch round cake pan with cooking spray and line with a round of parchment paper.

2 In a large bowl, whisk together the flour, baking powder, and salt.

3 In a medium bowl, whisk the ricotta, 1 cup/220g of the sugar, citrus zest (if using), the eggs, and vanilla until smooth. Whisk or gently fold into the flour mixture just until blended. Then fold in the melted butter, followed by half the raspberries, crushing them ever so slightly as you fold—you don't want them to disappear into the batter, just evenly distributed to create a nice, streaky look, almost like tie-dye.

4 Transfer the batter to the prepared pan and scatter the remaining raspberries and ¼ cup/55g sugar over the top. (It might look like a lot of sugar—it is! But it's necessary, promise.)

5 Bake until golden brown and a tester or toothpick inserted into the center comes out clean, 55–65 minutes. Let cool at least 20 minutes before unmolding.

almond cake with figs

Makes one 9-inch cake

Softened butter and sugar,
for the pan

1 cup/145g all-purpose flour

½ cup/60g almond or hazelnut
flour

1 teaspoon/4g baking powder

¾ teaspoon/3g kosher salt

1½ sticks/6 ounces/170g unsalted
butter, at room temperature

¾ cup/160g plus 2 tablespoons
sugar

½ vanilla bean, split lengthwise

2 large eggs

⅓ cup/80g Greek yogurt or
sour cream

1 pound/455g fresh figs, halved
or quartered if large (or rhubarb,
cut into 2-inch pieces or pears,
cored and quartered lengthwise)

Eat with
A large bowl of thick Greek
yogurt or labne with a drizzle of
honey, and a very good Riesling.

Do ahead
The cake can be baked 3 days
ahead and stored tightly
wrapped at room temperature.

If you're a part of the "Is this a cake or a tart" fan club (me), then you will love this cake. Yes, you're baking it in a tart pan, but I think the blurred distinction has more to do with the way the outside of this cake gets so crunchy and golden, almost like it's got a crust, while the inside stays rich, almost gooey. The almond flour keeps it moist, dense, and delightfully nutty while the figs provide jamminess without juiciness (putting that on a T-shirt). Feel free to go off-script with the fruit, as long as it isn't overly juicy. It's an already tender cake—excessive moisture will make it tough to bake through.

1   Preheat the oven to 350°F. Butter a 9-inch tart pan with a removable bottom and sprinkle with sugar, tapping out the excess. (Alternatively, line a 9-inch cake pan with a round of parchment and butter/sugar the paper.)

2   In a medium bowl, whisk together the flour, almond flour, baking powder, and salt.

3   In a stand mixer fitted with the paddle (or in a large bowl with an electric hand mixer), beat the butter and ¾ cup/160g of the sugar on high speed until it's super light and fluffy, about 4 minutes. Scrape in the seeds from the vanilla bean (saving the pod for another use; drop it in some vodka to infuse for your espresso martinis) and beat to blend.

4   Add the eggs, one at a time, beating on high until extremely pale and fluffy (almost reminiscent of Marshmallow Fluff), about 4 minutes.

5   Reduce the mixer speed to low and gradually add the flour mixture, then the yogurt. Beat, scraping down the sides of the bowl as needed, just to combine (the batter will be thick). Fold in about half the figs.

6   Scrape the batter into the prepared pan. Arrange the remaining figs over top, and sprinkle with the remaining 2 tablespoons sugar. Place the tart pan on a large sheet pan (to make it easier to remove) and bake, rotating the pan front to back once, until the cake is deeply golden brown and the figs on top are soft and beginning to brown, 65–75 minutes.

7   Let the cake cool before removing it from the pan.

brown butter pumpkin cake

Cooking spray

1½ sticks/6 ounces/170g unsalted butter

2 tablespoons/35g freshly grated ginger or 1½ teaspoons/3g ground ginger

2 teaspoons/4g ground cinnamon

½ teaspoon/1g ground nutmeg

1¾ cups/255g all-purpose flour

1 tablespoon/12g baking powder

1 teaspoon/6g baking soda

1½ teaspoons/6g kosher salt

1 (15-ounce/425g) can unsweetened pumpkin puree (about 1½ cups)

2 large eggs

1 cup/315g maple syrup

¾ cup/135g light brown sugar

Double recipe Salty Vanilla Frosting (optional; page 293)

For Frosted
it belongs at a chic autumnal dinner party. Unfrosted, it's your new favorite snacking cake.

Do ahead
The cake(s) or muffins can be baked 3 days ahead, tightly wrapped in plastic, and stored at room temperature.

This is one of the oldest recipes in one of my oldest recipe notebooks from the very first restaurant job I took, back in 2000. I've modified it to be makeable in a nonrestaurant setting (i.e., not as small teeny cakes baked in precious silicone molds), but it's still as perfect as ever. I'm a person who wouldn't consider myself thrilled about pumpkin or pumpkin-flavored things, but this cake really has a place in my heart. It's demurely spiced and not all that sweet, with a texture that anyone would be pleased to experience—simultaneously dense and spongy with an almost custardy texture thanks to the number of eggs and that whole can of pumpkin puree (you can make your own puree, but I'll join the chorus of bakers who will tell you it's simply not the same, nor is it better, than a can of Libby's).

1 Preheat the oven to 375°F. Spray one 9-inch cake pan or one 9 × 4-inch loaf pan with cooking spray and line with parchment paper. Or line 12 cups of a muffin tin with liners.

2 In a medium pot, melt the butter over medium-high heat and cook, swirling occasionally until the butter is browned, foamy, and smells like popcorn, 5–7 minutes. Remove from the heat and stir in the ginger, cinnamon, and nutmeg.

3 In a medium bowl, whisk together the flour, baking powder, baking soda, and salt.

4 In a large bowl, whisk the pumpkin puree, eggs, maple syrup, and brown sugar until combined. Slowly whisk in the flour mixture until nearly no lumps remain, followed immediately by the browned butter mixture, whisking until no lumps remain (the batter should be smooth and thick, but do not overmix).

5 Pour it into the prepared cake pan(s) or loaf pan, smoothing the top. Or divide among the muffin cups. Bake until golden brown on top, pulling away from the sides of the pan, and springing back lightly when pressed slightly: 25–30 minutes for cake pans, 65–75 minutes for a loaf pan, and 20–25 minutes for muffins. Let cool entirely before frosting, if you're going to frost (I like to frost!).

A single unfrosted cake would be elegant and perfect for snacking, a loaf cake is great for a week-long breakfast, and yes, sure, okay—you can turn these into muffins. But, while the original version of this cake never saw frosting (and it certainly doesn't need it), doubling the recipe and turning it into a layer cake with Salty Vanilla Frosting (page 293) is truly a chef's kiss moment.

toasted cake

Cake, warm out of the oven, is a wonderful thing. The butter still soft, everything fragrant and supple, not yet dried out from exposure to the outside world. Hard to argue with that sort of perfection. That is, unless you toast your cake. Then, one (me) would argue that it edges out warm cake as the Platonic ideal of perfection. Any sliceable cake (pound, loaf, you get the idea) over a day old (but especially as they inch toward day 3 or 4) will typically benefit from being toasted, either dry in a toaster oven, or sizzled in some butter, ghee, coconut oil, or olive oil (depending on the cake; let the flavor profiles guide you). It's got the same appeal of freshly baked cake with the added delight of a lightly crisped exterior, and increased flavor from toasting the flour and caramelizing the sugars inside.

While part of the beauty of most cakes is that they can sit on your countertop for a few days and somehow only get better with age, I will let you in on a secret: Cold, refrigerated cake, sliced extremely thin into delicate, nearly transparent sheets, is a fantastic treat. Sure, this is sort of the opposite of a fat slab of fluffy, just warm cake. And it's not a better experience, but a different, feathery one. You may think that the presence of butter would make the cake dry once chilled, but no. There's sour cream or yogurt, eggs, or oil (or some combination), that keep it rich and moist. Once refrigerated, the cake firms up in an extremely pleasant way, making it ideal for using a sharp or serrated knife to shave off a little at a time, all day long. A delicious, delicate snack.

cold cake

I like lining the pans with enough parchment overhang to make it easy to lift out.

(cottage) cheese cake with apricots

Makes one 9-inch cake

1 stick/4 ounces/115g unsalted butter

1¼ cups/180g all-purpose flour

2 teaspoons/8g baking powder

1 teaspoon/4g kosher salt

3 large eggs

2 cups/1 pound/455g cottage cheese or ricotta cheese

¾ cup/165g sugar, plus 2 tablespoons granulated sugar

½ cup/180g honey (or ½ cup/105g light brown sugar)

1½–2 pounds/680g–900g apricots, plums, rhubarb, bananas, or peaches, cut into slices about ½ inch thick

Eat with
This cake needs nothing, but serving with barely sweetened and lightly whipped cream plus a drizzle of honey is kinda nice.

Do ahead
The cake can be made 4 days ahead, and stored tightly wrapped at room temperature.

Note
One time, I was melting the butter for this cake and browned the butter by accident. It smelled so nice that I figured it would be wonderful in this cake, and it turns out, I was correct. But either works.

This is not a cheesecake (that's on page 138). It is a cake, made with cottage cheese. It is on the custardy side of things, so if you ever wished for something between a cheesecake and a cake, this cake might be the cake for you. Made in one bowl with any cut-up fruit you choose, it's as simple as the cake recipes in this book get. Out of the oven, it's slightly souffléd and has a dark brown, delightfully shiny top while staying impossibly delicate and custardy on the interior. My favorite thing about it: the little curds of cottage cheese that get caramelized at the bottom.

1 Preheat the oven to 400°F. Line a 9-inch cake pan (or springform pan) with parchment paper.

2 In a small saucepan, melt the butter over medium heat or brown it. I hate to give you this choice, but I'm telling you both work.

3 In a large bowl, whisk together the flour, baking powder, and salt.

4 In a medium bowl, whisk together the eggs, cottage cheese, ¾ cup/165g granulated sugar, and honey until combined. If using cottage cheese (as opposed to ricotta), you'll notice little cheese curds floating around— that's cool!

5 Begin to whisk the wet ingredients into the flour mixture and, just before it looks totally combined, add the melted (or browned) butter and whisk until it *is* totally combined. The batter will look a little lumpy (because of the cottage cheese) and perhaps a little loose. It is, after all, a cheese cake.

6 Using a spatula or wooden spoon, fold in about three-quarters of the fruit. Pour the batter into the prepared cake pan. Scatter the remaining fruit and the remaining 2 tablespoons of sugar over the top.

7 Bake until the cake is deeply (VERY deeply) browned on top, shiny, and no longer jiggly in the center, 45–55 minutes. The cake should appear puffed around the edges and spring back lightly when pressed.

8 Let cool completely before slicing.

This is the same cottage cheese cake as the one on the previous page (so nice, we photographed it twice!). Apricots, plums, and rhubarb are my favorites to use for their nice acidity and jammy texture once baked, but bananas are shockingly delicious in this cake as well.

chocolate–sour cream pound cake

Serves 8-10

1¼ cups/180g all-purpose flour

¾ cup/85g cocoa powder

1½ teaspoons/6g baking powder

1¾ teaspoons/7g kosher salt

1½ sticks/6 ounces/170g unsalted butter

1½ cups/330g granulated sugar

1 teaspoon/5g vanilla extract

2 large eggs

2 large egg yolks

1 cup/220g sour cream or whole-milk yogurt

8-10 ounces/225g-285g chocolate, chips or chopped-up bars (optional)

3 tablespoons demerara (or more granulated) sugar

Eat with
A dish of crème fraîche, or nothing at all.

Do ahead
The richness of this pound cake means it can last at least 5 days on the counter, tightly wrapped, up to 1 week refrigerated, or 1 month frozen.

For a person who's "not that into chocolate," it seems unlikely that I'd give valuable recipe real estate to another chocolate cake, when the other chocolate cake (page 112) does such a good job at being a chocolate cake. But this chocolate cake is a different thing altogether.

This chocolate cake, dense and buttery, deeply chocolaty, and studded with even more chunks of chocolate, is directly inspired by The Only Muffin I Have Ever Cared About: the chocolate-chocolate chip muffin from Costco. I've rewritten it to be a pound cake since, for whatever reason, I'm just no longer a MuffinPerson™ (although I'm sure this recipe would make for a great muffin). It's less for frosting and layering, more for slicing and snacking.

1   Preheat the oven to 350°F. Line a 9 × 4-inch loaf pan with parchment paper.

2   In a medium bowl, whisk together the flour, cocoa powder, baking powder, and salt.

3   In a stand mixer fitted with the paddle (or in a large bowl with an electric hand mixer), beat the butter, granulated sugar, and vanilla together until extremely pale and fluffy, 4–5 minutes. Scrape down the sides and add the whole eggs and egg yolks, one at a time, beating after each to incorporate. Continue beating until the mixture is smooth, fluffy, and well incorporated, 2–3 minutes.

4   With the mixer on low, add about half the flour mixture, followed by the sour cream, followed by the remaining half of the flour mixture (the idea being you don't want to add too much liquid to the egg mixture or it'll have a hard time incorporating, and you don't want to overmix the flour, which will give you a tough cake). Just before everything is incorporated, add three-quarters of the chocolate, if using.

5   Scrape the batter into the prepared pan, and sprinkle with the remaining chocolate (if using) and the demerara sugar. Bake until the cake is puffed, considerably taller, and pulling away from the sides of the pan, 65–75 minutes (pound cakes always take longer than you think).

6   Let cool entirely before removing from the pan.

extra coconut cake

Makes one tall 9-inch or a taller 8-inch cake

Cooking spray

2½ cups/360g all-purpose flour

2½ cups/225g unsweetened finely shredded coconut

1 tablespoon/12g baking powder

1¾ teaspoons/7g kosher salt

1½ cups/360g buttermilk

⅓ cup/70g melted coconut, grapeseed, or canola oil

1 teaspoon/5g vanilla extract

2½ sticks/10 ounces/285g unsalted butter, at room temperature, cut into 1-inch pieces

2 cups/440g sugar

4 large eggs

Salty Vanilla Frosting (page 293)

1 cup/110g unsweetened coconut chips, flakes, or more shredded coconut

Coconut cakes, are, by definition, extra. They should be tall and fuzzy like an obnoxious angora sweater. They are for parties, they are for celebrations, they are for keeping under a cake dome for you to cut thin slices off over the course of a full calendar week (I do not have a cake dome, but).

Part of the charm of the coconut cake is in the layering—the cake is sliced horizontally to expose the inside, which then gets covered in frosting. This produces an insanely rich, "moist" cake, with a good amount of frosting in each bite. If it were up to me, I would fill all my cakes this way (you can!). You, of course, do not have to do this— if slicing a cake like that makes you nervous, you can skip that step, just know your cake layers will be much thicker, with a different ratio of cake to frosting (but nevertheless delicious).

1 Preheat the oven to 325°F. Spray three 8-inch or two 9-inch cake pans with cooking spray and line with rounds of parchment.

2 In a medium bowl, whisk together the flour, coconut, baking powder, and salt.

3 In another medium bowl, whisk together the buttermilk, coconut oil, and vanilla.

4 In a stand mixer fitted with the paddle (or in a large bowl with an electric hand mixer), beat the butter and sugar together until extremely pale and fluffy, 4–5 minutes. Scrape down the sides and add the eggs, one at a time, beating well after each. Continue beating until the mixture is smooth, fluffy, and well incorporated, 2–3 minutes.

5 With the mixer on low, add about half the flour mixture, followed by the buttermilk mixture, followed by the remaining flour mixture (the idea being you don't want to add too much liquid to the egg mixture or it'll have a hard time incorporating, and you don't want to overmix the flour, which will give you a tough cake).

Eat with

This cake would be good after an equally "extra" meal, something like a giant ham or an abundantly large lasagna dinner. To serve, make sure you have some amaro handy. You'll want it.

Do ahead

The cakes themselves can be baked 2 days ahead, tightly wrapped in plastic, and stored at room temperature (or 3 days refrigerated). Frosted, the cake will last upwards of 5 days (I keep mine at room temperature, but a cold coconut cake is a thing of beauty).

6 Divide the batter evenly among the prepared pans and smooth the top. Bake until the cakes spring back lightly when touched at the top, look pale and blond on top and a nice golden brown on the sides, 30–35 minutes for the 9-inch and closer to 25–30 minutes for the 8-inch.

7 Let the cakes cool completely (either transfer them to a wire rack or let them cool in their pans), at least 1 hour at room temperature (do not rush the process by sticking them in the fridge).

8 If working with 9-inch cakes, use a long serrated knife to slice each one in half horizontally. It doesn't have to be perfect, nobody will notice if it's a little lopsided, I promise. If working with 8-inch cakes, you won't have to slice anything, just proceed to the next step.

9 Lay one layer (either the halved 9-inch or the whole 8-inch) on a plate lined with parchment (or not). Spoon ⅓–½ cup (for the four-layer 9-inch or three-layer 8-inch, respectively) frosting onto the layer and use an offset spatula, spoon, or butter knife to spread it into an even layer. Top with another layer of cake. (Tip: If your cake is "domed" more than you'd like, invert it, so the flat side is facing up, not down, creating a flat top) and repeat with more frosting. Repeat until you've used all the cake layers.

10 Once you get to the top, spread a thin layer of frosting all over the cake (this is known as a "crumb coat"—think of it as a primer), making sure to get into the sides and crevices created during the slicing/layering. Pop the cake into the fridge to set for 30–60 minutes (but leave the rest of the frosting at room temperature).

11 Meanwhile, in a medium skillet, gently toast the coconut flakes over medium heat, tossing constantly, just until they are lightly toasted and golden brown at the edges, 2–3 minutes. (If you like your coconut more brown/toasted, then do it! I prefer just a kiss of toasting, but that's personal preference.) Cool completely.

12 To finish the cake, spread the remaining frosting all over the sides and top of the cake. I want you to do the best you can, but also know you're about to cover it all up with coconut, so don't be too hard on yourself if it doesn't look incredible. Pat the coconut onto the sides of the cake until evenly covered, using the rest to sprinkle on top.

I do not really know how to frost a cake. Not well, anyway. But do you know what I can do, is smear frosting on the outside of a cake and cover it with flakes of gently toasted coconut (or sprinkles, or whatever you want to throw onto the sides of your cake to hide the fact that you, also, don't really know how to frost a cake). And then, it sort of looks like I know how to frost a cake? You know what they say, it's what's on the inside that counts.

citrusy cheesecake

Makes one 9-inch "cake"

For the crust

8 ounces/225g vanilla wafers or graham crackers

3 tablespoons/40g light brown sugar

6 tablespoons/3 ounces/85g unsalted butter, melted

Pinch of kosher salt

For the filling

2 (8-ounce/225g) packages cream cheese, at room temperature

1 cup/225g sour cream, whole-milk Greek yogurt, or labne

½ cup/110g granulated sugar

2 large eggs

2 tablespoons finely grated citrus zest (lemon, lime, tangerine, etc.)

Pinch of kosher salt

Thinly sliced citrus, for serving

Eat with
So much fresh citrus.

Do ahead
The cheesecake can be made 5 days ahead of time, tightly wrapped in plastic, and refrigerated.

Since cheesecake has a crust and a filling, does it belong in the cake chapter or the tart chapter? Cheesecake filling, with all that dairy and eggs, is kind of like a pudding, so maybe it could go there? These are the things that keep me up at night. But in the interest of being cheeky, it's here in the cake chapter (*cheese*cake, get it?). So sue me!

Before you continue reading, the two most important things you need to know about this cheesecake are (a) You don't need a water bath or springform pan to make it, (b) It's genuinely, truly, and completely foolproof. The man in this photo told me that, and I quote, "If you went on *Shark Tank* with this cheesecake as a business, they'd give you all your money," followed by, and again, I quote, "This cheesecake is better than Junior's, and I grew up in Brooklyn and I know cheesecake."

This cheesecake is slightly more citrusy than your average, almost Creamsicle-esque (Creamsicle: my favorite thing to eat and think about eating), but it could easily be tailored to a more classic flavor profile by simply using vanilla extract and omitting the zest. It's also the opposite of the classic tall, crustless New York-style: It's shorter and shallower, for a more fair crust-to-filling ratio and to eschew the whole bake-it-in-a-water-bath thing. To prevent it from cracking (a superficial thing that bothers some), cool the cheesecake at room temperature before refrigerating. (The drastic fluctuation in temperature is what causes the cracking! The more you know.) If it does crack, simply cover the top with a festive parade of your favorite sliced citrus.

1   **Make the crust:** Preheat the oven to 325°F.

2   In a food processor, pulse the cookies until you've got a good, coarse crumb (not too sandy or powdery). You can also do this by hand by placing the cookies in a resealable bag and crushing or smashing them with a rolling pin or heavy pot.

3   Transfer the crumbs to a medium bowl and add the brown sugar, melted butter, and salt. Using your hands, mix everything together until you've got a nice wet-sand texture with no obvious dry bits.

4 Press the crust into the bottom and up the sides of a 9-inch pie plate, tart pan, or springform pan. (Alternatively, you can use a 9-inch cake pan lined with parchment up the sides for easy removal.) Using the bottom of a measuring cup or small bowl, make sure the crust is really pressed in there, otherwise the cheesecake will be challenging to slice later once cooled.

5 Place the pan on a sheet pan (to make it easier to move in and out of the oven) and bake the crust until it's lightly golden brown at the edges (it gets baked again, so don't overdo it here), 10–12 minutes.

6 **Make the filling:** In a food processor, combine the cream cheese, sour cream, and granulated sugar. Blend the mixture, scraping down the sides to get all the bits, until it's extremely smooth, almost pudding-like in its texture. Add the eggs, citrus zest, and salt and continue to blend until there are no lumps (this is your last chance to remove lumps!) and the mixture is smooth and nearly liquefied.

7 Pour the filling into the prepared crust, stopping just before it reaches the top of the crust (you may have some leftover filling depending on your chosen vessel). Bake until the filling is mostly set with just a small, slight jiggle in the center (and absolutely no browning!), 25–30 minutes. Turn the oven off and leave the door open a crack—let the cheesecake sit inside the oven as it gradually cools for about 20 minutes.

8 Remove from the oven to cool at room temperature before transferring it to the fridge to cool completely (about 2 hours). This annoying sequence is optional, but it is good at preventing those deep cracks that form from sudden temperature change.

9 Scatter fresh citrus slices on top as you like before slicing and serving.

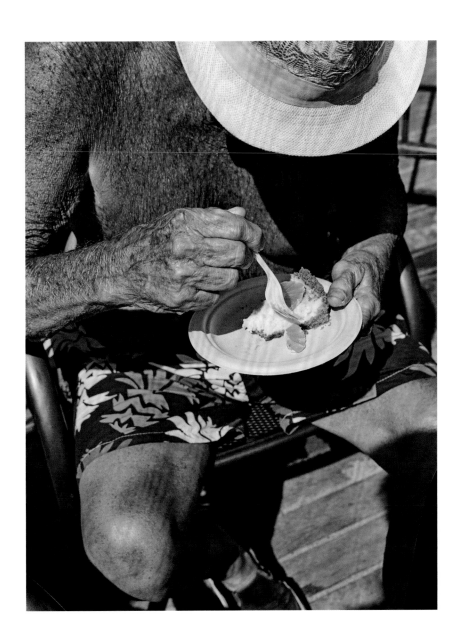

golden ginger cake

Makes one 9-inch cake

Cooking spray or softened butter, for the pan

Demerara or granulated sugar, for the pan and batter

2¾ cups/400g all-purpose flour

1 tablespoon/6g ground turmeric

1½ teaspoons/6g kosher salt

1 teaspoon/2g ground cinnamon

1½ teaspoons/6g baking powder

1 teaspoon/6g baking soda

1½ sticks/6 ounces/170g unsalted butter, at room temperature

1 cup/210g light brown sugar

¼ cup/80g molasses

3 tablespoons/50g finely grated fresh ginger

2 large eggs

½ cup/120g buttermilk

¼ cup/50g vegetable or melted coconut oil

Eat with
A bottle of amaro.

Do ahead
The cake can be baked 2-3 days ahead, tightly wrapped in plastic, and stored at room temperature. After day 3, it would greatly benefit from a quick toast in a buttered skillet before eating.

If you've ever wished one of those ginger molasses cookies was a cake, well, have I got the cake for you. It's holiday-festive, but I could very well see this cake turning up at afternoon teas or late lunches, or just be made to sit on your countertop, for you to take a sliver every time you walk by. A friend described it as "a quiet, dignified cake," having "good springiness," with the turmeric adding a "pleasant mustiness, like finding yourself alone in the back halls of a museum on a sunny day." Took the words right out of my mouth.

1 Preheat the oven to 350°F. Spray a 9-inch springform pan or cake pan with cooking spray (or grease with softened butter) and sprinkle with a bit of sugar to coat the interior of the pan. Tap out the excess.

2 In a medium bowl, whisk together the flour, turmeric, salt, cinnamon, baking powder, and baking soda.

3 In a stand mixer fitted with the paddle (or in a large bowl with an electric hand mixer), beat together the butter, brown sugar, molasses, and fresh ginger until the mixture is light, fluffy, and the color of a very pale latte, 3–4 minutes. (Periodically scrape down the sides of the bowl with a spatula to make sure all the ingredients are mixing properly.)

4 Add the eggs, one at a time, until the mixture looks extremely light and fluffy, almost like cake frosting, 5 or so minutes. It might look a little broken or separated, but the mixture will come together, promise.

5 In a medium bowl, combine the buttermilk and oil. With the mixer on low, beat one-third of the flour mixture into the cake batter, followed by half of the buttermilk mixture. Repeat with one-third of the flour mixture, the remaining buttermilk mixture, and remaining flour

6 Pour the cake batter into the prepared pan and scatter with enough demerara sugar to lightly cover the top. Bake, rotating the pan front to back once or twice, until the cake has started to pull away from the sides of the pan, is evenly golden brown on top, and it springs back ever so slightly when pressed, 50–55 minutes. Let the cake cool completely before unmolding on a wire rack if you have one. (If not, just let it cool away from the oven.)

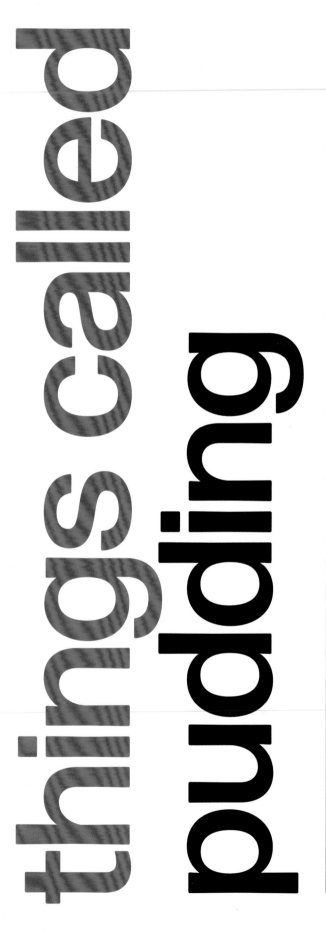

things called pudding

The word pudding *is loosely translated across many cultures and countries, meaning many things in different places. In America and other parts of the world, it's typically defined as a dairy or custard (dairy combined with egg) thickened with a starch like cornstarch, semolina, cornmeal, or rice. In the UK and other Commonwealth countries, it simply means ... dessert. Regardless of how it's defined, it's always one of the most fun things to eat and even more fun to say.*

The recipes in this chapter reflect the variety of definitions given, but the one thing they have in common is their pleasant softness. For as much as I exalt crunchiness, crispiness, and flakiness, there is something undeniably comforting about something that's purely smooth, gentle, and uncomplicated. It is admittedly challenging (or at least annoying) to make pudding in any quantity other than "a lot," and for that reason, it's one of the best desserts to make when feeding a crowd (or just like to have a week's worth of dessert at the ready). Serve your pudding of choice from one giant bowl with several small spoons, divided among your favorite small coupes you've been struggling to find a use for, or directly out of the pot it was cooked in. Even those who don't have room for much else will always find room for pudding.

plummy pudding

Serves 4-6

1 cup/150g all-purpose flour

¼ cup/55g sugar,
plus 2 tablespoons for sprinkling

¼ cup/50g light brown sugar

2 teaspoons/9g baking powder

¾ teaspoon/3g kosher salt

3 large eggs

¾ cup/175g whole milk

½ teaspoon/2g vanilla extract or
½ vanilla bean, split lengthwise

4 tablespoons/2 ounces/55g
unsalted butter, melted

1½ pounds/680g plums
(or peaches, nectarines, apricots,
or cherries), cut into 1-inch wedges,
or 1 pound/455g blackberries,
whole, or strawberries, hulled
and quartered

Eat with
A bowl of Greek yogurt or
whipped cream and a glass of
red vermouth on ice.

Do ahead
If you can avoid it, don't. While
still delicious after sitting for a
few hours, this dessert is truly
best eaten the minute it comes
out of the oven. The batter is not
worth making ahead, since it
comes together so quickly.

A great example of really taking advantage of the vagueness of the word *pudding*, this dessert is nearly unclassifiable, but the taste is all the same familiar. It would be a clafoutis if it were denser. It would be a cobbler if it were more like a sliceable cake. It could be a bread pudding with fruit instead of bread. Whatever it is, it's one of my favorite ways to use up leftover fruit, the type that's so ripe and perfect, it needs little more than a buttery batter poured around it, containing just enough flour to simply absorb the juices of the fruit as it roasts inside a custardy bath. While it's near impossible to mess up, the only tragedy would be to use underripe or out-of-season fruit— it bakes so quickly, there's not much time for the fruit to soften, should that be required. Otherwise: foolproof.

For those who "don't bake," well, you just haven't baked this yet.

1 Preheat the oven to 425°F.

2 In a large bowl, whisk together the flour, ¼ cup/55g of the sugar, the brown sugar, baking powder, and salt.

3 In a medium bowl, whisk together the eggs, milk, and vanilla extract (or scrape in the vanilla seeds; save the pod for another use). Add this to the flour mixture, mixing just to blend until you see no lumps, followed by the melted butter.

4 Cover the bottom of a 2–3-quart (or liter) baking dish with the fruit and sprinkle with the remaining 2 tablespoons sugar. Pour the batter over the fruit and bake until the top is deeply golden brown and puffed around the edges, 25–30 minutes (it should still be slightly custardy in the center). Let cool slightly before eating.

hot buttered rum pudding

Makes 4 cups/serves 8-10

6 tablespoons/3 ounces/85g unsalted butter

1 vanilla bean, split lengthwise, or 1 teaspoon vanilla extract

3 tablespoons/36g dark rum or bourbon

1½ cups/360g heavy cream

1½ cups/360g whole milk

Pinch of kosher salt

5 large egg yolks

½ cup/65g cornstarch

¼ cup/55g granulated sugar

½ cup/105g light brown sugar

Whipped cream, crème fraîche, 50/50 (Tangy Whipped Cream, page 279) or mascarpone, for serving

Eat with
Crumbled-up gingersnaps or Nilla wafers, mounds of whipped cream, an amaro on ice.

Do ahead
This pudding can stay in your fridge, covered tightly, for up to 5 days.

The year is 2000. You're inside a dark bar that calls itself a "speakeasy," despite having an address on Google Maps. A mustachio'd person wearing suspenders asks if you'd like to try the "Hot Buttered Rum." He laughs. Of course, this isn't your typical Hot Buttered Rum, he says. There is—he glances sideways, then back to meet your gaze—a twist!

Have I ever had a Hot Buttered Rum? No. But I imagine something that tastes of butterscotch, laced with rum, made with brown sugar and toasted vanilla. That sounds good, right? So if you've had Hot Buttered Rum, consider this my twist. If you haven't, well, consider this a great butterscotch pudding that has rum inside it.

1 In a small skillet or saucepan, melt the butter over medium-high heat until browned. If using the vanilla bean, scrape in the seeds and cook, swirling occasionally, until the butter smells like toasted nuts or popcorn, or add vanilla extract. Add the rum and remove from the heat.

2 In a medium pot, heat the cream, milk, and salt over medium heat until it comes to a simmer. Remove from the heat.

3 In a heatproof medium bowl, whisk together the egg yolks, cornstarch, and granulated sugar until light and pale. Gently whisk in some of the hot cream mixture until about half is incorporated. Transfer the warmed egg yolk mixture to the pot with the remaining dairy and cook over medium heat, whisking constantly, until the mixture starts to bubble and thicken, 15–18 minutes.

4 Whisk in the butter/rum mixture, followed by the brown sugar, until no lumps remain, all the butter is incorporated, and the sugar is dissolved.

5 Remove from the heat and divide among small bowls or place in one large bowl. Cover with plastic wrap and refrigerate until totally set, at least 2 hours.

summer pudding with summer fruit

Serves 6

1 pound/455g peaches, nectarines, or apricots, cut into slices 1 inch thick

⅓ cup/70g granulated sugar, plus more for sprinkling

2 teaspoons finely grated fresh ginger (optional)

¾ pound/340g blackberries or raspberries, plus an extra handful for garnish

1 cup/220g heavy cream

2 tablespoons powdered sugar

½ cup/145g whole-milk Greek yogurt or labne

½ loaf brioche, challah, pain de mie, Pullman loaf, or Japanese milk bread,* crusts removed and sliced 1 inch thick

*Basically any loaf of white or enriched bread will do. Oh, and take it from me: Presliced white bread, while tempting, is too thin and will not give you the structure and stability this pudding requires.

My instincts had me sold on the concept of "summer pudding" before I even fully knew what it was, simply because the name was so damn charming. When I found out that one of the main ingredients in this popular British dessert (pudding) is "a loaf of white bread," I knew my instincts had led me to a good place, and when I figured out there was also smushed, ripe, jammy fruit, I knew it was a GREAT place. If you can't imagine what those things together might taste like, think of it as using the white bread as a sort of unsweetened cake, soaking up the sugary juices of said jammy fruit. Although not customary, I like to layer mine with some tangy whipped cream so that after some time in the fridge, it sets up to a spoonable, vaguely sliceable parfait-style dessert, not unlike a fruit-based tiramisu.

While it's on the fussier side of the spectrum (two fruits to cook, one whip, not inconsiderable refrigeration time, the instructions are long), in my defense, it doesn't require any actual baking, you really can't mess it up, and it's a total babe of a dessert. Plus: It's fun! Because good God, sometimes it's nice to just make something that screams FUN, no? It's also a good one to make when there's no oven, or maybe you simply don't want to turn yours on. While I enjoy this smaller version, it really is impressive to double the recipe and make a giant version in a 9-inch springform pan (could anything be more FUN?).

1   In a medium pot, combine the peaches, half the granulated sugar, and the ginger (if using) and bring to a simmer over medium heat. Cook, swirling occasionally, until the peaches have started to release their juices (but are not turning into jam), 8–10 minutes. Remove from the heat and transfer to a medium bowl. Set aside to cool.

2   Without rinsing out the pot, combine the berries and remaining half of the granulated sugar. Bring to a simmer over medium heat and cook, swirling occasionally, until the berries have started to release their juices (but are not turning into jam), 8–10 minutes. Remove from the heat and transfer to a medium bowl, separate from the peaches. Set aside to cool completely.

3   Meanwhile, in a large bowl with a whisk , beat the cream and powdered sugar until spreadable, pillowy, medium peaks form. (You can also do this with an electric hand mixer.) Whisk in the yogurt until well blended.

Because this is a cookbook and I need to provide clear instructions, I call for a 6-inch cake pan or any bowl with a 6-cup capacity (most small-medium mixing bowls fit the bill), but do not feel beholden to that structure. At the risk of being too vague, you can pretty much use whatever you want as long as there are sides and it holds everything inside.

Eat with

A giant Arnold Palmer in the sun, a "fun" wine, or something with bubbles.

Do ahead

The fruit mixtures can be made 1 week ahead of time. The summer pudding can be assembled 3 days ahead (do not take out of the mold if you can help it), wrapped tightly in plastic, and refrigerated.

4 Line a 6-inch cake pan or a bowl with at least a 6-cup capacity (see note at left) with plastic wrap so that there is ample overhang. (If doubling the recipe, use a 9-inch cake pan/9-inch springform pan or two bowls/small cake pans.)

5 Place one layer of sliced bread on the bottom of the pan or bowl. Cut the bread to fit as needed to make sure there is an even layer with no obvious gaps (aesthetics don't matter here, as it'll be covered up).

6 Spoon about one-third of the berry juices (a few spoonfuls—just eyeball it) onto the bread to thoroughly soak, followed by half of the berries themselves. Spoon one-third of the peach juices onto the bread and berries, followed by half of the peaches themselves.

7 Spread one-third of the cream mixture onto the fruit and top with another layer of bread, making sure to fill any obvious gaps with bread that's cut to fit. Top the bread with another one-third of the berry juices and all of the remaining berries, followed by one-third of the peach juices and all of the remaining peaches. Top with one-third of the cream mixture, setting the remaining cream mixture aside in the refrigerator.

8 Place another layer of bread on top, making sure to fill any obvious gaps, especially around the edges, with bread that's cut to fit. Spoon the remaining fruit juices on top, making sure to stain the entire surface. Place a piece of plastic wrap on top and then place a plate on top of the plastic. Rest a heavy can (or another medium-size, relatively heavy, food-safe object) on top to lightly compress the whole shebang. Refrigerate for at least 4 hours.

9 Before serving, crush a handful of berries with a sprinkling of sugar and let sit for a few minutes to release the juices. Remove the springform sides and plastic wrap. (If using a regular cake pan or a bowl, place the pudding on a large plate and invert it, then remove the plastic wrap.) If using a cake pan, I like to top the pudding with the remaining cream mixture, swirling in the crushed berries to create streaks and swirls, almost like I'm frosting it. If I made it in a bowl, I'll likely simply serve the remaining cream and berries on the side. Wherever your journey leads you, slice (or spoon) the pudding and serve.

a bowl of salted chocolate pudding

Makes 4 cups/serves 4-6

5 ounces/140g bittersweet chocolate (65%-70% cacao), finely chopped

1½ cups/360g heavy cream

1½ cups/360g whole milk

¼ cup/28g unsweetened cocoa powder

¾ cup/165g granulated sugar

3 large egg yolks

¼ cup/30g cornstarch

1 teaspoon/4g kosher salt

1 teaspoon/5g vanilla extract

50/50 (Tangy Whipped Cream, page 279)

Flaky sea salt, for serving

Cookies, such as chocolate wafers or gingersnaps, for crumbling or dipping

Eat with
At the end of your next gathering, when the lights are low and the music is loud and you think you've run out of wine but find that one extra bottle in the back of the fridge—that's the moment to bring out the bowl of chocolate pudding.

Do ahead
Chocolate pudding is proudly sturdy and can stay in your fridge, covered tightly, for up to 5 days.

Not unlike the vanilla pudding (aka Vanilla Pastry Cream, page 158), this salted chocolate pudding should be left alone, simply celebrated for what it is, which is a bowl of melted chocolate made spoonable and consumable by a LOT of dairy (plus some sugar, egg yolks, and cornstarch, as is customary for pudding). My favorite way to consume this sexy, hedonistic number is not in dainty little cups—no, this pudding wants to be served in a giant bowl, topped with a tangy yogurt- or sour cream-laced whipped cream and lots of flaky salt with nothing but a handful of spoons for individual indulging. No personal bowls, no serving utensils. This giant bowl of silky chocolate is meant to be shared with friends and lovers. (Alternatively, use it to make friends and lovers—works every time.)

1   Place the chocolate in a large heatproof bowl.

2   In a medium pot, heat the heavy cream, milk, cocoa powder, and 6 tablespoons of the sugar over medium-high heat, whisking constantly until the mixture comes to a bare simmer, 8–10 minutes. Remove from the heat.

3   In a separate large bowl, whisk together the remaining 6 tablespoons sugar, the egg yolks, cornstarch, salt, and vanilla until the mixture is lump-free and pale in color. Whisking constantly, ladle a bit of the hot cream mixture into the egg yolks and whisk until completely blended. Add a little bit more at a time, until half the cream mixture is combined with the egg yolk mixture. Transfer the yolk/cream mixture to the pot with the remaining cream mixture.

4   Return the pot to medium heat and, whisking constantly, cook until the mixture has gone from thin and watery to thick and custardy, with the occasional bubble popping up, 3–5 minutes.

5   Immediately pour the hot mixture over the chocolate and let sit for a minute or two, giving the bowl a shake to help the chocolate settle as it melts. Whisk the mixture until you have an ultrasmooth, silky pudding. Transfer to a flat baking dish (an 8 × 8-inch pan works well) and cover with plastic wrap directly on the surface of the pudding. Refrigerate until the pudding is completely set, at least 3 hours, and up to 48 hours.

vanilla pastry cream, a perfect pudding

*Makes about 5 cups**

4 cups/945g whole milk

1 cup/220g sugar

1 vanilla bean, split lengthwise, or 1½ teaspoons/7g vanilla extract

8 large egg yolks

½ cup/65g cornstarch

1 teaspoon/4g kosher salt

4 tablespoons/2 ounces/60g unsalted butter

*This makes enough for 6-8 people as its own special dessert, or to assemble a casual trifle (see page 95), or to fill a tart, like Caramelized Vanilla Custard Tart (page 26) or Simple Fruit Tart (page 25).

Do ahead
Vanilla pastry cream is proudly sturdy and can stay in your fridge, covered tightly, for up to 5 days.

Use for
To serve as perfect pudding, pour it into serving glasses, cups, coupes, bowls, whatever you fancy. Top with whipped cream or leave as is. After all, it is perfect. Or use it to build a casual trifle or fill a tart (see pages 25, 26, and 95). Or spread onto cake, fill éclairs or cream puffs (no recipe here for those, but if you have one, fill away!), or fold with whipped cream to make it lighter. And it's perfectly delicious used as a layer in a tiramisu.

We tend to take the simplest things for granted, or think of them as boring. "But what ELSE is there?" you might ask when presented with the option of eating a bowl of perfect vanilla pudding. We're constantly looking for MORE and DIFFERENT, and might forget that milk and cream sweetened with a bit of sugar, flavored with vanilla, enriched with egg yolks, thickened with cornstarch, and set with a healthy knob of butter is as close to paradise on this wild planet as you can get. Traditionally used to fill things (tarts, éclairs, etc.), pastry cream is always billed as a means to an end, but for me, this thick, velvety vanilla custard *is* the end. That's it, that's the dessert, perfect as is.

1 In a medium pot, combine the milk and ½ cup/110g of the sugar. If using the vanilla bean, scrape the seeds into the milk and add the pod, too (if using vanilla extract, it goes in later). Bring to a simmer over medium heat, but do not let it boil. Once simmering, remove from the heat.

2 Meanwhile, in a medium bowl, whisk the remaining ½ cup/110g sugar with the egg yolks, cornstarch, vanilla extract (if using), and salt.

3 Slowly pour a cup of the hot milk mixture into the egg yolk mixture while whisking and whisk to blend. Do this until all the milk has been incorporated. The mixture will be loose with a starchy texture.

4 Return this mixture to the pot and place over medium heat. Whisk constantly, cooking until the liquid goes from thin with many small bubbles, almost like a cappuccino, to thick and gelatinous with sporadic large bubbles, bubbling from the great depths of the pot, 8–10 minutes. The mixture will have gone from soupy liquid to golden pudding faster than you think. Magic! Remove from the heat and whisk in the butter.

5 Transfer the pudding to a shallow baking dish or bowl and place a piece of plastic wrap or parchment paper directly on top (to prevent the "skin"). Place in the fridge and chill completely until ready to use.

6 When ready to serve or use, transfer the mixture to a large bowl and whisk until it goes from thick and rubbery to creamy, luscious, and smooth.

As close to paradise on this wild planet as you can get.

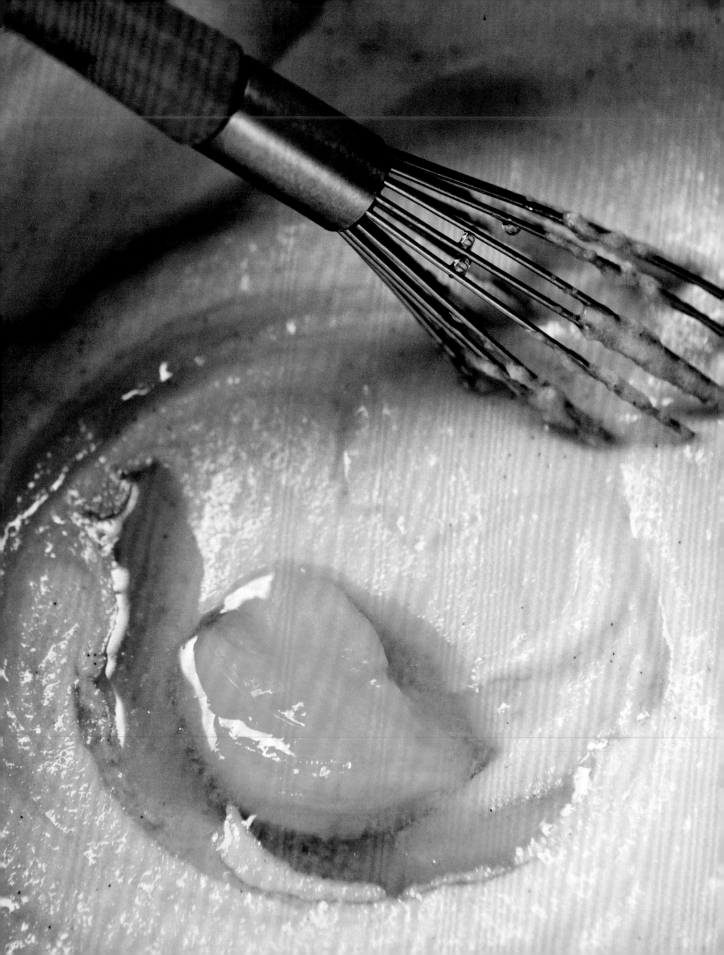

milk and honey semolina pudding

4 cups/945ml whole milk

½ cup/180ml honey, plus more to taste and for serving

1 vanilla bean, split lengthwise (optional)

Pinch of kosher salt

¾ cup/110g semolina flour

3 tablespoons /1½ ounces/45g unsalted butter, cut into small pieces, plus more for serving

Flaky sea salt

Eat with

Lots of honey and sliced fresh or roasted fruit. A good pour of cold cream or whole milk on top would also be great.

Do ahead

This can be made several hours ahead of time, but you may want to add a splash of milk or water upon reheating.

Semolina pudding is popular as a dessert in many countries throughout Europe and the Middle East but has yet to "become a thing" in the USA. Oh, what's semolina, exactly? I'm so glad you asked. It's a coarse wheat flour ground specifically from the durum variety of wheat. In addition to being coarser, it's got a nuttier, earthier flavor with an occasionally golden hue, looking almost like fine cornmeal.

When cooked with milk and honey, it acts as a thickener, taking on a porridge-y, casual Cream of Wheat vibe, which makes sense because both things are, in fact, semolina cooked in milk or water and lightly sweetened. (Thanks to the BIG CEREAL industrial complex, Cream of Wheat = healthy, nutritious breakfast. Semolina pudding = dessert.) It's easy, deceptively classy, and very, very chic. I would eat this out of the pot with nothing else (I have done this), but it's also nice spooned into individual bowls and topped with chunky jam, hard roasted fruit (like on page 217), or gorgeous naked peaches (page 228). To me, semolina pudding is the easier, quicker version of rice pudding: a comforting, basic dessert that appeals to the child within, which my therapist tells me is desperately in need of some parenting.

1   In a medium saucepan, combine the milk, 1 cup/240ml water, the honey, and kosher salt. If using the vanilla, scrape in the seeds (save the pod for another use). Bring to a bare simmer over medium heat (do not boil). Reduce the heat to low and whisk in the semolina a little bit at a time.

2   Keep whisking whisking whisking, making sure you're getting the bottom of the pot, until the mixture looks thick, like porridge, 10–15 minutes. Whisk in the butter, followed by more honey to taste.

3   Divide among bowls and serve with another little pat of butter, a drizzle of honey, and sprinkle of flaky salt.

2 cups sugar + 1 cup unsalted butter + 2½ cups whole milk + 1 13-ounce can evaporated milk (I love this), + 2 tablespoons grated nutmeg (okay, this seems like a lot) + 2 tablespoons vanilla extract (again, feels like extra) + 1 loaf wet (?) bread + 1 cup raisins (not for me, but I'll do whatever she says) and some softened butter, for greasing the dish, and "hard sauce," for serving (which I take to mean the classic mid-century combo of softened butter mixed with powdered sugar and booze) + Cream the butter and sugar, add both the milks, nutmeg and vanilla + Stir this mixture into the wet bread, add raisins, stir and pour into a greased baking dish + Bake at 350° for 2 hours, stirring halfway.

nora ephron's bread pudding

These are the notes I took for a bread pudding recipe that I cobbled together from my favorite Nora Ephron book, *Heartburn*. It's a tour-de-force 1983 novel about many things, but chiefly, love and divorce in New York. (There is the iconic film as well, starring Meryl Streep and Jack Nicholson. While I think the book is better than the film, both are gorgeous, vulnerable pieces of art worth experiencing.) The novel is laced with secret recipes authored by the protagonist, Rachel Samstat, a cookbook author, as she describes the dissolution of her marriage to a person who too closely resembles my thorniest ex.

Aside from me talking about this book to anyone who wants to listen, this bread pudding did intrigue me. It seemed less like bread pudding and more like milky, caramelized hunks of bread? Which I will say, sounded weird and fantastic and just the sort of thing I wanted to eat. Anyway, before I even knew what the table of contents for this book was going to be, I knew that I wanted to find a way to put in a Nora Ephron recipe that she herself already gave to us in one of her books. It would be a wink, an homage to one of my favorite writers, a woman I am sad I never got to share a martini with at Keens Steakhouse.

Of all the recipes she mentions in that book, bread pudding was an unexpected one to attach myself to. Truthfully, I don't even like it all that much. But I *am* nevertheless attached. We made it often during my professional pastry chef days, not so much as a dessert for the menu (maybe a little too unrefined for our fine-dining atmosphere), but for family meal (the meal the staff ate together before service began). There were always hunks of bread about to go to waste, egg yolks left over from something else, dairy close to an expiration date. Bread pudding was a cheap, scalable dessert that pleased nearly everyone—an almost impossible task. We baked it in giant hotel pans, chilled it, sliced it into cubes, and rewarmed them for a treat at the end of our little meal, eaten out of plastic deli containers while squatting on milk crates.

That style of eating followed me into every kitchen I worked. No matter the place, you ate out of plastic containers, sitting on a milk crate. Against a wall. In a circle. In the event there were actual chairs available, it was still always a race to occupy the milk crates, lest someone sitting in a chair be judged for, I don't know, "taking it easy" or something. "Must be nice, sitting in a real chair, while I'm down on this milk crate," etc. Family meal, as a practice, often felt like a 24-minute game of passive-aggressive martyr-chicken. Who would be the last to come, so that someone would notice they didn't get any food? Who could sit in the most uncomfortable position on the shittiest milk crate for the shortest amount of time? Who would be the person to eat the fastest so they could get back to work, to demonstrate they had the most work to do?

As a member of The Pastry Department, we were the least respected and the most dismissed, but still, we made everyone bread pudding. Imagine being treated like shit every day but still showing up with a full hotel pan of warm, custardy dessert. Maybe we just wanted to be liked, and everyone knows a great way to be liked is to show up with something delicious. Is this why I got into cooking? Lots to unpack.

Anyway, Nora Ephron's bread pudding. I made this dessert once, twice. And you know what, I thought it was . . . good. It tasted just as I had thought it might judging by the ingredient list and (vague) instructions: caramelized, chewy bits of bread stuck to one another with intense sweetness. No softness from the typical egg yolk-laced custard I had come to know as a key element of bread pudding. This was something else altogether, almost like a dry, caramelized tres leches. I liked it, but it wasn't bread pudding to me, and I couldn't figure out an occasion that seemed appropriate to serve it. Maybe it didn't have a home here in this book, except maybe to tell you this story, but that's okay by me.

toasted rice pudding

Makes 5 cups/serves 4-6

1 cinnamon stick or ¼ teaspoon ground cinnamon

⅓ cup/70g long-grain (jasmine, basmati, or Jasmati) rice

3 cups/720g whole milk (or unsweetened oat or almond milk, extra creamy if available)

½ cup/110g sugar

1 vanilla bean, split lengthwise, or ½ teaspoon vanilla extract (optional)

Pinch of kosher salt

2 egg yolks (optional)

Eat with
Something crunchy on top, a dusting of cinnamon, a dollop of whipped cream, or splash of cold cream. Or enjoy all alone out of the fridge in your nighttime clothes.

Do ahead
Rice pudding can be made 5 days ahead, stored covered tightly with plastic wrap, and refrigerated.

Note
The egg yolks are optional since I know some folks are uncomfortable with eating semicooked eggs—but they do add a nice custardy note. My preference? I love it both ways, which is why I couldn't commit (story of my life).

People who love rice pudding would truly and absolutely die for it. That fact alone made my exploration of this dessert a little fraught. Is it best served warm? Cold? Cinnamon optional? Egg yolks added? Could I please everyone? Of course not. But I could please myself.

This rice pudding is inspired by my first rice pudding memory: Kozy Shack cups at my aunt's house down the Jersey Shore. And listen, is this rice pudding better that Kozy Shack eaten at the Jersey Shore? I can't say that it is. But it's pretty great. And I think you'll love it (but only if you love rice pudding).

Try to release your fear when the rice pudding is looser than you think it ought to be when going into the fridge (in this house, rice pudding is chilled). It will thicken as it cools, in this you must trust.

1   In a medium pot, combine the rice and cinnamon stick (if using; ground cinnamon goes in later) and toast over medium-high heat, stirring constantly, until the grains of rice smell slightly toasty and turn a barely perceptible shade of golden brown, 4–5 minutes.

2   Add the milk, sugar, 2 cups/480g water, and salt. If using, scrape in the vanilla seeds (throw in the pod or save it to dry), or add the vanilla extract. Bring to a simmer over medium heat, then reduce the heat to medium-low and continue simmering until the rice is totally cooked through and tender and you notice the liquid beginning to thicken up, 20–25 minutes (the rice will still be intact, almost swimming in a liquid, but the liquid itself will be starchy, able to coat the back of a spoon).

3   Reduce the heat to low and continue to stir constantly, making sure no grains of rice stick to the bottom of the pot while encouraging the starch to release from the grains and into the liquid (not unlike risotto). Continue simmering until the rice is beyond tender (but not mush) and the mixture appears pudding-like, another 15–20 minutes.

4   Remove the pudding from the heat and whisk in the egg yolks (if using), stirring to cook them slightly. Transfer the pudding to serving cups, bowls, or coupes, or one giant bowl, whatever you like. If you like warm rice pudding, you can eat it now. Otherwise, place plastic wrap directly on the surface and let it chill completely in the refrigerator.

If you overthink it, this dessert immediately becomes less fun.

salted cookies and cream parfait

Let me tell you about the first recipe I ever developed. When I was little, I took ballet, tap, and "jazz" classes, something I'm sure nobody would guess if they knew me as an adult. Every Saturday I'd put on my powder-pink leotard, matching tights, and small ballet slippers and fill a cereal bowl full of Crispix. Just before I'd get into my mom's Jeep and head to class, I'd pour milk over the Crispix and leave the house. About two hours later, I'd come back to a perfect bowl of mushy, milk-soaked cereal. That's it. That's the recipe.

We all gotta start somewhere, right? Anyway, it's a shining example of something crunchy intentionally made softer for someone's enjoyment, not unlike dunking biscotti into espresso, French fries into milkshake, or an Oreo into milk. This all brings me here, to this "pudding."

Crunchy chocolate wafer cookies are layered with dollops of salty whipped cream, softening as they sit, creating a sort of "pudding" texture (how this dessert ended up in this chapter). Cookies and cream ice cream but not frozen, one million Oreos dunked in milk—it's a great DIY version of something you already know you loved.

It's admittedly kind of silly, barely qualifying as a recipe. But it really does taste so, so good. Less meant to be sliced and more meant to be scooped, this can be made in any vessel that has sides and fits in your fridge and is ideal for any moment where you need dessert but lack the skills or desire for baking.

In a large bowl with a whisk or an electric hand mixer, whisk **2 cups/ 460g heavy cream** with ¼ **cup/30g powdered sugar** until you've got gorgeous, medium-stiff peaks. Season this with a **good pinch of salt**.

Line a 9 × 4-inch loaf pan, 8-inch cake pan, medium bowl (mixing, serving, whatever), or whatever vessel you have with plastic wrap. Spoon a bit of whipped cream onto the bottom, just enough to create a nice even layer. Take a **few chocolate wafer cookies** and place them on top of the cream or coarsely crush them and sprinkle them (once they've softened into the cream, it almost doesn't matter how they're put in—but this first layer is what you'll see on the outside).

Follow with another even layer of whipped cream and a layer of cookies. Repeat until you've filled the vessel or run out of cookies or whipped cream, whichever comes first, but try to end with a nice, thin layer of the whipped cream. I hate to be so vague, but what can I say, this really is that casual. If you overthink it, this dessert immediately becomes less fun, so let's stay on task here.

Place a piece of plastic wrap directly on top of the last layer and press gently to encourage everything to compress slightly. Refrigerate for at least 2 hours, until everything becomes nicely softened and able to be spooned.

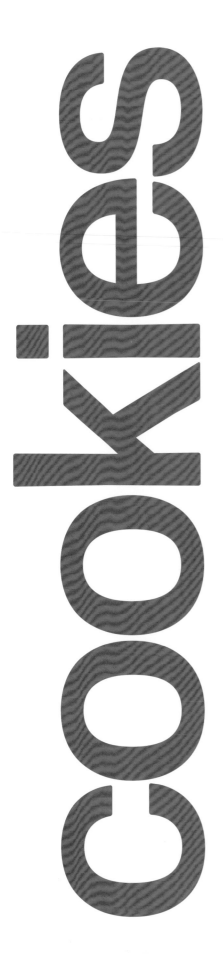

cookies

During the development of this book, I had to really examine my personal hierarchy of desserts. As it turns out, most cookies fall to the bottom of my list, which may be the least popular thing I've ever said. That being true, shortbread remains at the top of the heap because, well, I contain multitudes of recipes. So in accordance with that hot take, the following recipes are mostly shortbread, and the ones that aren't, are close enough to still make the cut.

What follows in this chapter are, to me, perfect cookies. Flexible and versatile, able to be made nutty or chocolaty, salty or sweet, crunchy or tender, cut small and thick or sliced large and thin. They are the definition of "a little something," a perfect small treat, always just the thing. Some of the recipes might seem a little basic, but ideally, you take that freedom and do with it what you will, knowing you're starting from a very good, reliable base source.

Because I like to be upfront, there aren't any warm-out-of-the-oven, ooey-gooey moments here. The deliciousness of these cookies lies in their crunchy edges, the tender crumb, the perfect snap, and the just-sweet-enough dough coated in crystalline sugar to create balance. Shortbread is also not only one of the only cookies, but desserts period, that get better with age. As they sit, the butter continues to tenderize the toasted flour, the salt gets to season deeply and well, and a day later, you'll find yourself even more in love with what was already pretty perfect to begin with.

salted pistachio shortbread

Makes 24 cookies

Cooking spray or softened butter, for the pan

¾ cup/95g pistachios, almonds, hazelnuts, or walnuts

½ cup/60g powdered sugar, plus more for dusting

1 stick/4 ounces/115g cold unsalted butter, cut into 1-inch pieces

½ teaspoon/2g kosher salt

¾ cup/110g all-purpose flour

Flaky sea salt

Eat with
A good runny, soft, creamy cheese, a bowl of Castelvetrano olives, and a glass of chilled sherry.

Do ahead
The dough can be made 5 days ahead, tightly wrapped, and refrigerated. The cookies can be baked 3 days ahead and stored airtight at room temperature.

This is a sturdy shortbread cookie, unapologetically nutty, appealing to anyone who wants "a little sweet something" without committing to a classically dessert-y cookie. It's a lovely snack, salty and crumbly in all the right places. For those who don't want to shell a million pistachios—please don't!—shelled pistachios are widely available in the bulk section of any store that has one, and increasingly more popular as a packaged good. If you strike out, feel free to use any of the other nuts suggested below, either raw or roasted, but always unsalted (there's enough salt in the dough, promise!).

1 Preheat the oven to 350°F. Lightly grease a 9-inch springform pan or tart pan with a removable bottom with cooking spray or softened butter and line the bottom with a round of parchment paper.

2 In a food processor, process the pistachios until finely ground. Remove 2 tablespoons and set aside.

3 Add the powdered sugar, butter, and salt to the food processor and pulse until well combined. Add the flour and process until a slightly sticky dough forms (if your food processor is having trouble and the dough still looks "sandy," just dump the dough out onto a counter and mix it by hand until a gorgeous dough forms—it will come together!).

4 Press the dough into the prepared pan into an even layer (you can use your hands, or use the bottom of a measuring cup to press) and sprinkle with the reserved 2 tablespoons ground pistachios and some flaky salt.

5 Bake until the cookie is just golden around the edges and dough is baked through, 15–20 minutes.

6 Once the cookie is out of the oven, remove it from the pan. Dust it with more powdered sugar, if you like that visual energy. While the dough is still warm (but not too hot to handle), slice the cookie into 24 thin wedges (start by cutting the round into quarters, then slice each quarter in half, then each half into thirds to get nice, thin triangles).

7 Let the cookies cool completely before transferring them (they will be soft and easily broken if moved before cooled).

cinnamon sandies

Makes 24 cookies

1¼ cups/130g walnuts or pecans

1¾ cups/255g all-purpose flour

1¼ teaspoons/5g kosher salt

2 teaspoons/4g ground cinnamon

2 sticks/8 ounces/225g unsalted butter, cut into 1-inch pieces, at room temperature

⅓ cup/40g powdered sugar

¼ cup/50g light brown sugar

1 teaspoon/5g vanilla extract

¾ cup/165g granulated sugar

1 large egg

Flaky sea salt

Eat with
Eggnog? Feels right.

Do ahead
The cookies can be baked 4 days ahead and stored airtight at room temperature.

Note
Alternatively, you could skip the egg wash and sugaring, just slice and bake the naked discs, and dip each baked cookie into a bowl of powdered sugar, à la Mexican wedding cookies. Also very good!

These lightly spiced, buttery, crumbly, crunchy cookies are somewhere between a tender shortbread, a bizcochito, and a Mexican wedding cookie. Nuts contribute to their rich-yet-sandy texture, so if you are allergic, sadly I would recommend another cookie. The roll-in-sugar really does so, so, so much for the texture (so crisp!) and boosting the sweetness (the dough isn't that sweet), so please, don't skip.

1   In a food processor, pulse together the nuts, flour, kosher salt, and 1 teaspoon cinnamon until the nuts are ground, but not a total powder. Transfer to a medium bowl. (Alternatively, very, very finely chop the nuts and add to a bowl with the flour, salt, and 1 teaspoon cinnamon.)

2   Add the butter, powdered sugar, brown sugar, vanilla, and ¼ cup/55g of the granulated sugar to the food processor and process until smooth. (Alternatively, beat the ingredients in a stand mixer on medium-high until smooth and fluffy, 3–5 minutes.)

3   Add the nut/flour mixture to the food processor (or mixer) and pulse (or mix) just to combine. You should have a slightly crumbly dough that will soften as soon as you start to mold it with your hands.

4   Turn the dough out onto a surface and knead it a few times until it comes together, like Play-Doh. Form it into a log 2 inches in diameter.

5   Wrap the dough in plastic wrap or parchment paper, rolling it to encourage a round, cylindrical shape. Refrigerate for at least 2 hours.

6   Preheat the oven to 350°F. Line two baking sheets with parchment paper. Beat the egg with about a teaspoon of water to make an egg wash.

7   In a loaf pan, baking dish, or any long vessel with sides, mix the remaining ½ cup/110g granulated sugar and 1 teaspoon cinnamon together. Brush the log with the egg wash and roll it in the cinnamon sugar. Slice cookies about ⅛ inch and place them on the lined baking sheets.

8   Sprinkle each cookie with flaky salt and bake until the edges are lightly browned and your kitchen smells like it's inside a box of Cinnamon Toast Crunch, 10–12 minutes. Remove from the oven and let cool completely.

perfect salted shortbread

Makes 30–40 cookies

2½ sticks/10 ounces/285g cold salted butter,* cut into 1-inch pieces

½ cup/110g granulated sugar, plus more for rolling

⅓ cup/70g light brown sugar

1 teaspoon/5g vanilla extract

2¼ cups/325g all-purpose flour

1 large egg

Flaky sea salt

*If using unsalted butter, add 1¼ teaspoons/5g kosher salt to the mixer when beating the butter and sugar.

Eat with
Anything and anyone.
Every party, every baby shower, every picnic, every class reunion, every parent-teacher conference, every stoop sale.

Do ahead
The cookie dough can be made 5 days ahead, tightly wrapped, and refrigerated (or 1 month ahead, tightly wrapped and frozen). The cookies can be baked 3 days ahead and stored airtight at room temperature.

Shortbread is a perfect cookie. Buttery, tender yet crumbly, a little salty, and made with only a few ingredients, most of which you likely have on hand. It can be modified to suit your needs and desires by adding things like chocolate chunks, ground cinnamon, toasted nuts, lemon zest—whatever. This here is the most basic version, a simple, sublime buttery cookie that truly holds its own and always seems welcome no matter the occasion, just like a bag of salty potato chips.

1 In a stand mixer fitted with the paddle (or in a medium bowl with an electric hand mixer or food processor), beat the butter, both sugars, and the vanilla on medium-high until it's super light and fluffy, 3–5 minutes. Using a spatula, scrape down the sides of the bowl and, with the mixer on low, slowly add the flour and beat just to blend.

2 Divide the dough into four even pieces, placing each on a large piece of plastic wrap. Fold the plastic over so that it covers the dough to protect your hands from getting sticky. Using your hands (just like you're playing with clay), form each piece of dough into a log shape, about 1¼-ish inches in diameter. (I like these cookies thicker and smaller-in-diameter, like little fat, buttery coins.) Rolling the dough on the counter will help you smooth it out, but don't worry about getting it totally perfect. (You can also do this using parchment paper, if you prefer.) Refrigerate until totally firm, about 2 hours.

3 Preheat the oven to 350°F. Line a baking sheet or two with parchment paper. Beat the egg with 1 teaspoon of water for your egg wash.

4 Brush the outside of the logs with the egg wash and roll them in more granulated sugar (for those really delicious crispy edges).

5 Slice each log into ½-inch-thick rounds, place them on the lined baking sheet(s) about 1 inch apart, and sprinkle with flaky salt.

6 Bake until the edges are just beginning to brown and the whole cookie looks sparkly and gorgeously golden, 12–15 minutes. Let cool completely before eating them all (trust me, a warm cookie is great, but a room-temperature shortbread is better).

crunchy chocolate shortbread

Makes 24 cookies

2 cups/290g all-purpose flour

⅔ cup/75g cocoa powder

2½ sticks/10 ounces/285g cold salted butter,* cut into 1-inch pieces

½ cup/110g granulated sugar

⅓ cup/70g light brown sugar

1 teaspoon/5g vanilla extract

8 ounces/225g chocolate (65%–72% cacao), roughly chopped

1 cup/100g unsalted roasted nuts, such as hazelnuts, peanuts, walnuts, or almonds, roughly chopped (optional)

½ cup/65g white sesame seeds, toasted (optional)

Demerara sugar, for rolling

1 large egg

Flaky sea salt

*If no salted butter is available, use unsalted butter plus 1 teaspoon/4g kosher salt.

Eat with
A giant glass of cold milk.

Do ahead
The dough can be made 5 days ahead, tightly wrapped, and refrigerated (or 1 month ahead, tightly wrapped and frozen). The cookies can be baked 3 days ahead, and stored airtight at room temperature.

If you ever made the salted butter chocolate chunk shortbread from my first cookbook, *Dining In* (2017!), and thought "I sure wish these were all chocolate," then you will want to make these. (They are these.)

1   In a medium bowl, whisk together the flour and cocoa powder.

2   In a stand mixer fitted with the paddle (or in a medium bowl with an electric hand mixer or bowl of a food processor), beat the butter, both sugars, and vanilla on medium-high until it's super light and fluffy, 3–5 minutes.

3   Using a spatula, scrape down the sides of the bowl and, with the mixer on low, slowly add the flour mixture, followed by the chocolate chunks plus any desired nuts or seeds, and beat just to blend.

4   Divide the dough in half, placing each piece on a large piece of plastic wrap. Fold the plastic over so that it covers the dough to protect your hands from getting sticky. Using your hands (just like you're playing with clay), form each piece of dough into a log shape, about 2-ish inches in diameter. (I like these cookies thinner but larger-in-diameter, like a crispy, snappier cookie.) Rolling the dough on the counter will help you smooth it out, but don't worry about getting it totally perfect. (You can also do this using parchment paper, if you prefer.) Refrigerate until totally firm, about 2 hours.

5   Preheat the oven to 350°F. Line a baking sheet or two with parchment paper. Beat the egg with about 1 teaspoon of water for your egg wash.

6   Brush the outside of the logs with the egg wash and roll them in the demerara sugar (for those really delicious crispy edges).

7   Slice each log into ⅛–¼-inch-thick rounds, place them on the lined baking sheet(s) about 1 inch apart, and sprinkle with flaky salt.

8   Bake until the sugared edges are nicely browned, all lacy and crispy looking, 12–15 minutes. Let cool completely before eating them all (trust me, a warm cookie is great, but a room-temperature shortbread is better).

salty lemon shortbread

Makes 24 cookies

Finely grated zest of 3 lemons

½ cup/110g plus 2 tablespoons/
25g granulated sugar

Flaky sea salt

1 stick/4 ounces/113.5g cold
unsalted butter, cut into 1-inch
pieces

¼ cup/30g powdered sugar

½ preserved lemon (optional),
seeded and finely chopped

¾ teaspoons/3g kosher salt

1 teaspoon/5g vanilla extract

1 cup/145g all-purpose flour

Eat with
A bunch of juicy grapes at a very
lovely picnic, hot coffee.

Do ahead
The dough can be made 5 days
ahead, tightly wrapped, and
refrigerated (or 1 month ahead,
tightly wrapped and frozen).
The cookies can be baked 3 days
ahead and stored airtight at
room temperature.

Just as I made sure to get anchovies into this book (see page 71), preserved lemons were bound to show up sooner or later. Sure, they are optional here (there's plenty of salt and lemon in this recipe to justify the name even without their inclusion), but they really do produce a jammy, salty, floral bop of something spectacular when you bite into a piece of one while nibbling on this otherwise straightforward cookie. Don't forget the sugar on top; the dough itself really isn't sweet enough to carry the cookie without it, plus, the way the zest gets a little crisp and dried along with it . . . it's a real chef's kiss.

1   Preheat the oven to 350°F. Line an 8-inch round cake pan or 8 × 8-inch baking dish with parchment paper.

2   In a small bowl. combine one-third of the grated zest, 2 tablespoons sugar, and a good pinch of flaky salt. Use your fingers to rub the mixture together until the sugar is tinted yellow and smells deeply of lemon. Set aside.

3   In a stand mixer fitted with the paddle (or in a medium bowl with an electric hand mixer or bowl of a food processor), beat the butter, powdered sugar, the remaining ½ cup/110g granulated sugar, the remaining lemon zest, preserved lemon (if using), kosher salt, and vanilla on medium-high until light and fluffy, 3–5 minutes. Using a spatula, scrape down the sides of the bowl and, with the mixer on low, slowly add the flour and beat just to blend.

4   Pat the dough into the prepared pan, using your palm or the bottom of a measuring cup to flatten to the best of your ability. Using the tines of a fork, dock/prick the top of the shortbread dough. Sprinkle the top with the lemon-rubbed sugar, pressing it into the raw dough.

5   Bake until the edges are just beginning to brown and the dough is set and firm to touch (but still slightly malleable), 20–25 minutes.

6   After about 10 minutes of resting, the cookie should be firm enough to handle and lift out of the pan, but still warm enough to slice. Remove the one large cookie from the pan and, using a knife, cut into 1-inch wedges or 1 × 3-inch bars. Let cool completely before eating them all (trust me, a warm cookie is great, but a room-temperature shortbread is better).

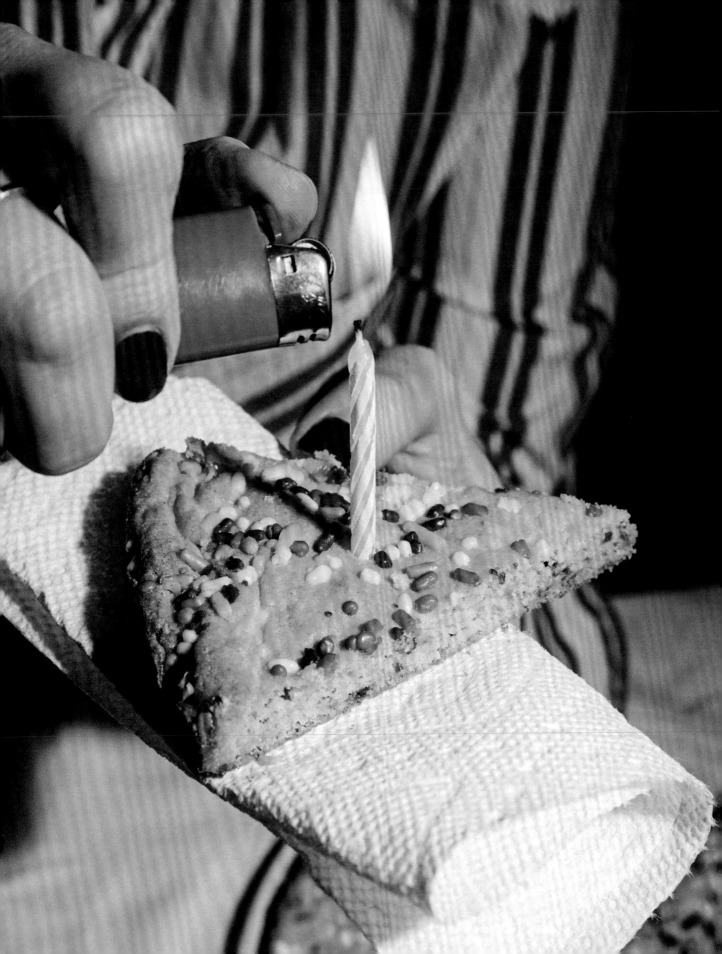

birthday cookies

Makes 32 cookies

6 large egg yolks

¾ cup/150g sugar

1 teaspoon/5g vanilla extract

1½ sticks/6 ounces/170g unsalted butter, cut into ½-inch pieces, at room temperature

1½ cups/220g all-purpose flour

⅓ cup/75g sprinkles, plus 4 tablespoons, for the top

1 tablespoon/12g baking powder

1 teaspoon/4g kosher salt

Flaky sea salt

Do ahead
The dough can be made 5 days ahead, tightly wrapped and refrigerated (or 1 month ahead, tightly wrapped and frozen). The cookies can be baked 3 days ahead and stored airtight at room temperature.

Birthday cake isn't in everyone's baking wheelhouse, which I get. Or maybe it's not in the realm of possibilities because there simply aren't enough hours in the day to measure, mix, bake, cool, and frost something. Or maybe you need to bring a birthday dessert somewhere and you need something you're confident won't smush, squash, or melt. Well, then, allow me to introduce you to these cookies. They taste like birthday cake, only take 30-ish minutes to make, and look cute sliced into triangles with a candle stuck inside. Bake them, birthday or not.

1 Preheat the oven to 350°F. Line an 8- or 9-inch cake pan with a round of parchment paper (or, if baking two, line two pans).

2 In a stand mixer fitted with the paddle (or in a medium bowl with an electric hand mixer), beat the yolks, sugar, and vanilla together on medium speed until extremely pale and fluffy, looking almost like hollandaise or aioli, 4–5 minutes.

3 With the mixer running, add the butter a few pieces at a time, waiting until the little pieces fully incorporate into the yolk mixture before adding more. Continue adding until all the butter is incorporated and your mixture is pale and smooth, another 4–5 minutes.

4 In a medium bowl, whisk together the flour, ⅓ cup/75g sprinkles, the baking powder, and kosher salt. With the mixer on low, add the flour mixture to the buttery yolks, beating just to blend.

5 Divide the dough in half, refrigerate whatever you aren't planning on baking. Pat one disc of the dough into the lined cake pan and sprinkle with 2 tablespoons of sprinkles and a bit of flaky salt.

6 Bake until shiny, golden brown, and slightly puffed on top (it will look like a very flat birthday cake), 20–25 minutes (if you like yours on the softer, chewier side, bake closer to 20 minutes).

7 Remove the cookie from the oven and let it cool slightly before transferring it to a cutting board and slicing it into little wedges (you can do this in the pan as well, but I try to avoid doing that lest I scratch the surface of my cake pan). Repeat with the other disc of dough, now or later.

black and white cookies, or, my favorite sugar cookie

Makes 24 cookies

For the cookies

3¼ cups/470g all-purpose flour, plus more for rolling

1¼ teaspoons/5g kosher salt

1 teaspoon/4g baking powder

3 sticks/12 ounces/340g unsalted butter, cut into 1-inch pieces, at room temperature

1 cup/220g granulated sugar

⅓ cup/40g powdered sugar

1 teaspoon/5g vanilla extract

1 large egg

1 large egg yolk

For the icing and assembly

3 large egg whites

1 teaspoon lemon juice

3¾ cups/450g powdered sugar

1 cup/112g black sesame seeds, toasted (optional; or food coloring, sprinkles, etc.)

Do ahead
The cookie dough can be made 5 days ahead, wrapped tightly, and refrigerated. The cookies can be baked 2-3 days ahead and stored airtight at room temperature, or up to 1 month ahead, wrapped very well, and frozen.

Everyone needs a good sugar cookie recipe, and this is mine. I hate to do it a disservice by describing this as the most boring cookie in the world, but sugar cookies are a little boring, and that's okay. It's their purpose to be practical and stable, a building block of your baking repertoire, like a good white T-shirt in your wardrobe. It's happy to melt into the background, to let the loudness of a sprinkle or several drops of food coloring receive all the attention.

These cookies are sweet-ish, but not so sweet that they can't take a blanket of frosting (and they should). They of course have plenty of salt, and just enough vanilla to remind you of those Danish butter cookies that come in a blue tin (which, incidentally, can be approximated here with this dough, see below). They're buttery but not sandy, snappy but not too crisp, slightly supple but not cake-y. Just be sure not to roll them too thin (liable to break) or too thick (nobody wants to eat that much of a sugar cookie).

1 **Make the cookies:** In a medium bowl, whisk together the flour, salt, and baking powder.

2 In a stand mixer fitted with the paddle (or in a large bowl with an electric hand mixer), beat the butter, granulated sugar, powdered sugar, and vanilla together on medium-high until light and fluffy, 3–5 minutes. Add the whole egg, followed by the egg yolk, scraping down the sides of the bowl as needed to incorporate everything (especially the butter and sugar at the bottom of the bowl).

3 With the mixer on low, add the flour mixture and beat just to blend, again, paying attention to the sandy parts at the bottom of the bowl.

4 Divide the dough into two balls and wrap each piece in plastic wrap, patting it into a nice, flat disc. Refrigerate for at least 1 hour.

5 Preheat the oven to 350°F. Line one or two baking sheets with parchment.

6 On a lightly floured work surface, roll one disc of dough at a time to about ⅛ inch thick. Cut out shapes to your heart's desire and transfer to the lined baking sheet(s). Gather up any scraps, pat together, re-roll, and cut out more cookies. (Do this two times, max, or wrap the dough and save it in the fridge for later.)

When it comes to decoration, the world is truly your oyster. For example, here, I've made these into an homage to the terrible/wonderful black and white cookies from Zabar's, a cheeky nod using black sesame seeds cemented with a classic royal icing. But in classic flexible fashion, please do make these your own, swapping the seeds for sprinkles or skipping them and simply tinting the icing with your favorite color.

7 Bake, rotating the pan front to back once, until the cookies are lightly golden brown at the edges, but still fairly pale toward the center, 12–15 minutes. They should puff slightly but still hold their shape.

8 Remove the pan from the oven and transfer the cookies to a wire rack to cool completely and quickly (they will firm up as they cool).

9 **Make the icing:** In a stand mixer fitted with the whisk (or in a large bowl with an electric hand mixer), beat the egg whites on high speed until light and fluffy, 2–3 minutes. Add the lemon juice and slowly beat in the powdered sugar. Beat on high until you've got a supremely light, fluffy mixture, looking like Marshmallow Fluff or shaving cream. To get it to proper consistency, whisk in 2 tablespoons water. The icing should be spoonable and spread slightly when piped—to test this, spoon a little bit onto a plate. If it's too runny (too much spreading), add more powdered sugar. If it's too thick (no spreading), add water, a tiny spoonful at a time. If you want to tint the icing, add a few drops of food coloring (I prefer gel food coloring over liquid).

10 Place about 1 cup of icing in a sandwich-size zip-top plastic bag (roll the opening down to make it easier to fill, and resist the urge to overfill). Snip a teeny hole in one corner and squeeze the icing toward the hole.

11 Ice each cookie as you wish. For the black and white cookies pictured, draw a circle around the outside of the cookie with the icing. Fill in half of the circle with icing and immediately sprinkle on the black sesame seeds, tapping off the excess. Fill in the other half of the circle with icing. Let the icing dry at least 20 minutes before eating.

To make faux linzers: While not the real deal, adding 1 teaspoon ground cinnamon to the dough will give you a lightly spiced cookie, good for sandwiching with raspberry jam (see page 238) like a little faux linzer.

To make Danish butter cookies: Punch out a smaller circle in the center of your dough round to make a wreath shape. Dust in coarse sanding sugar before baking and skip the icing.

frozen

things

My freezer always has at least one pint of mint chip ice cream at all times—it's the only dessert I keep on hand. I grew up eating frozen yogurt with sprinkles as a reward for any time I did anything well in school, and worked at Jamba Juice as a teenager consuming a steady diet of what was basically pureed ice cream and fruit juice. So, you could say I've always made it my business to indulge in cold, frozen desserts. They're the style of dessert I will always have room for at the end of even the largest meal, the style of dessert that I will want for every birthday (specifically, mint chip ice cream cake, and no, I'll never suggest making your own ice cream because it simply will never be better than what you can buy, sorry).

I'll level with you and say that most of the recipes here are "mixed" or "assembled" more than "made," which will either bore you or thrill you, but I hope you're thrilled. Most need only three or four ingredients and a few hours (for freezing) and effectively zero "baking": frozen melon with crushed raspberries, Creamsicle made with fresh citrus, and, of course, ice cream cakes (with and without actual cake).

frozen melon with crushed berries

Serves 6–8

1 pound 6 ounces/625g melon (about 1 cantaloupe or ½ small watermelon)

½ cup/120g fresh lemon or lime juice, plus more to taste

2 tablespoons sugar or honey, plus more to taste

2 cups/9 ounces/255g raspberries or blackberries

Flaky sea salt, sumac, and/or Aleppo chile flakes (optional)

Eat with
Potato chips dipped in ranch, preferably floating in a pool inside something inflatable. A true fantasy!

Do ahead
The frozen melon mixture can be frozen up to 1 month ahead, if you want, just make sure it's wrapped tightly. Scraped, it lasts about 1 week before needing a re-fluff.

Somewhere between the texture of a sharp, icy granita and creamy Italian ice, lies this frozen melon. Since it's made with the whole fruit, with basically no dilution except for a little citrus juice, it's got a nice melon-y flavor and plenty of familiar melon-y texture, but it's, you know, frozen. It's a great solution to the question on everyone's mind come August: What am I supposed to do with all this melon? And I do mean *all* the melon. Cantaloupe, watermelon, canary, yellow seedless—this application is perfect for any and all abundant melons that come your way.

When blending the melon, keep it chunkier than you think. A food processor is good for that, albeit messy—I like to use a blender and just pulse, rather than blend.

1   In a blender or food processor, combine the melon, lemon juice, and sugar and blend until mostly but not entirely smooth (melon always stays a little chunky; that's okay, it's why we like it). Season with more citrus juice and sweetener, if it needs it. The mixture should be on the tart-ish side and a little sweeter than you'd like (flavors dull the colder they are, so keep that in mind).

2   Pour the mixture into a loaf pan, baking dish, cake pan, whatever you have. Wrap it in plastic if you don't plan on eating this for a few days. Freeze until solid, at least 2 hours, depending on your freezer. Once solid, remove it from the freezer and scatter a few berries over the top. Using a spoon or fork, scrape the whole mixture, crushing the fresh fruit as you go, to create a slushie-like texture. Return it to the freezer for another 30 minutes or so to firm up.

3   Fluff up the mixture again (a fork is really best for this) and spoon it into glasses or small bowls for serving, alongside more fresh fruit (berries or melon). Sprinkle with big flaky salt, sumac, and/or Aleppo chile flakes if you'd like.

very iced, very frozen coffee

Serves 6–8

4 cups/945g strong brewed coffee (cool or cold)

¼–½ cup/55g–110g plus 2 tablespoons/25g sugar

¼ cup/50g vodka, coffee liqueur, Baileys, or bourbon (optional)

¾ cup/175g heavy cream

¾ cup/6 ounces/170g mascarpone

Kosher salt

Eat with
A plate of Perfect Salted Shortbread (page 176) or Cinnamon Sandies (page 174) and an additional shot of vodka or other alcohol of your choice.

Do ahead
The coffee mixture can be frozen up to 1 month ahead, if you want, just make sure it's wrapped tightly. Scraped, it lasts about 1 week before needing a re-fluff.

There is not a better thing to end a meal with than a tiny espresso, but you know who doesn't want to make an espresso after dinner? Me. I don't even own an espresso maker, so I couldn't even if I wanted to. But I do have a freezer, and this dessert is the next best thing, sometimes even better. With a cloud kiss of whipped mascarpone dolloped just so, I feel like a special little barista every time I serve it.

And before you ask "Is this an espresso martini?" know that . . . sure, yes, but also no. While I do love to serve this in festive coupes or martini glasses, the alcohol isn't here to "get you drunk." Rather, alcohol lowers the temperature at which liquids freeze, meaning this treat is always the perfect texture for scraping into tiny little frozen crystals à la granita, and not, say, a solid block of coffee ice. If you're skipping the alcohol, it'll still be great, but just be prepared for a bit more elbow grease when scraping the frozen coffee.

1 In a medium bowl, combine the coffee, ¼ cup/55g of the sugar, and the vodka (if using), and stir to dissolve the sugar. Taste it—if you like your coffee on the sweeter side, feel free to add the remaining ¼ cup/55g sugar, or maybe if you're using a sweet liqueur, like Kahlúa, you might not need it. (It's okay if it tastes a little too sweet prefreeze; flavors dull the colder they are.)

2 Pour the mixture into a loaf pan, cake pan, shallow baking dish, whatever, and place in the freezer. Wait for it to freeze (at least 2 hours, depending on your freezer), then use a fork to scrape up the frozen coffee into little fluffy crystals.

3 When ready to serve, in a medium bowl, with a whisk or an electric hand mixer, whisk the heavy cream with the remaining 2 tablespoons/25g sugar until medium-stiff peaks form. Whisk in the mascarpone and a small pinch of salt.

4 I like to spoon some of the frozen coffee into a martini glass or coupe, then sort of compact the crystals so they are dense but still edible with a spoon. Top with a perfect little dollop of the whipped mascarpone.

banana split
ice cream cake

Serves 10–16

For the banana jam

¾ cup/165g granulated sugar

4 large bananas, cut into 1-inch chunks

¼ cup/60g heavy cream

Kosher salt

For assembly

3 pints/1.5 liters vanilla ice cream

1 (9-ounce/255g) box chocolate wafer cookies

2 cups/475g heavy cream

¼ cup/30g powdered sugar

Maraschino cherries, for fun

Eat with
Many friends
(seriously, this ice cream cake serves a lot of people).

Do ahead
The banana jam can be made 2 weeks ahead and stored airtight in the refrigerator. The ice cream cake can be assembled 1 week ahead, tightly wrapped in plastic, and frozen.

I fed this to someone who has eaten a lot of my food over the years and his first comment was "WOW, this is . . . incredible." His second comment was: "This SO does not seem like you." I asked why and he suggested that it looked and tasted much fussier, elaborate, and fancy than anything I typically enjoy making or eating. He forgot "whimsical, silly, playful, and Pinterest-y." And he's not wrong! We all have surprises.

Aside from the fact that I genuinely think this is one of the best-tasting, most fun-to-eat desserts I've ever made, the other surprise here is that this ice cream cake doesn't actually take that much effort, more just time (to freeze) and space (in your freezer). The caramel banana jam alone is worth the journey, and it's something I think you might want to have on hand to put on your ice cream in the future, even if there is no ice cream cake assembly involved.

1   **Make the banana jam:** In a small (ideally heavy-bottomed) pot, cook the granulated sugar over medium heat. Use a heatproof spatula to stir occasionally, until the sugar starts to dissolve and then eventually caramelize, turning a delightfully golden graham cracker brown color, 3–4 minutes. (This is known as a "dry" caramel, where there is no water involved. For more on that, see page 288.)

2   Add the bananas and stir to coat in the caramel (the sugar will bubble up and start to seize a bit, that's okay, it'll smooth out). Cook the bananas, stirring occasionally, for about a minute or so, until they start to look broken down and jammy. Add the heavy cream, season with salt, and remove from the heat. Cool completely.

3   **To assemble:** Place the ice cream on your counter to soften for a few minutes—you want the texture to be slightly softer than simply "scoopable," but decidedly not "melted." Meanwhile, coarsely crush the chocolate wafers by hand (not too fine). Line a 9-inch springform cake pan with plastic wrap, making sure there's some plastic wrap hanging over the edges.

4   Scatter half the cookies on the bottom and cover with half the ice cream. Use your palms to smush the ice cream down, making sure it's in one even layer (you could use a spoon, but I feel like using your hands is faster and honestly more fun). Spread the banana jam on top of the ice cream, followed by the rest of the ice cream.

5   Scatter the remaining crushed cookies on top of the ice cream, pressing them in to make one even layer (it should come to the top of the springform pan). Place in the freezer until extremely firm, at least 3 hours, depending on your freezer (this one likes to be very solid before slicing, if you can wait).

6   Meanwhile, in a bowl with a whisk or an electric hand mixer, beat the heavy cream to medium peaks, then whisk in the powdered sugar. Beat until you've got nice pillowy stiff peaks. Refrigerate the whipped cream until ready to serve.

7   When you're ready to serve, carefully unmold the ice cream cake—if it still feels a little too mushy/malleable for your liking, pop it back into the freezer until it feels solid enough to exist without its frame.

8   Once the cake is frozen and ready, remove the springform sides and frost the outside and the top once more with the whipped cream. This can be put back into the freezer, if you like, or sliced and served as is. Serve each slice with an additional dollop of whipped cream and a maraschino cherry on top (for fun).

festive frozen yogurt (with sprinkles!)

Serves 6-8

1 cup/230g heavy cream

2 cups/460g whole-milk yogurt (Greek or otherwise)

¾ cup/235g maple syrup

¾ cup/170g fresh lemon juice

1 teaspoon vanilla extract

Pinch of salt

3 tablespoons sprinkles or jam (store-bought or any from pages 238-239)

Ice cream cones (optional), for serving

* I know it seems like a silly tool, but I use my ice cream scoop all the time (I eat a lot of ice cream), and having one will make scooping this seem all the more festive.

Eat with
So many hot dogs.

Do ahead
Frozen yogurt can be made 2 weeks ahead and stored airtight in the freezer.

Sure, you can go to a "froyo" store and get a really excellent pull of creamy, frozen something that tastes of yogurt (but is too good for it to be just yogurt). Trust me, I grew up going to Humphrey Yogart (yes, *that* Humphrey Yogart, the one Meghan Markle worked at, and no, we never met), slamming cones of vanilla with rainbow sprinkles my whole life— it's a perfect food. But times have changed, and last time I "went out for frozen yogurt" I waited in line for forty-two minutes behind a line of rowdy teens creating content. 3/10, would not do again!

So if you, too, refuse to wait in line for that long, then this recipe is for you. You won't get that iconic swirly moment, more of a scoop-vibe, but you also won't have to leave the house or wait in line with a group of humans two generations below you, forcing you to reckon with your own mortality. Point being, making, serving, and eating this tangy, luscious frozen yogurt generously flecked with sprinkles (!) is a fully fun experience. Your own frozen yogurt? What a delight.

1 In a medium bowl, with a whisk or an electric hand mixer, whisk the heavy cream to medium-stiff peaks.

2 In a separate bowl, whisk together the yogurt, maple syrup, lemon juice, vanilla, and salt. Gently fold the whipped cream into the yogurt mixture, followed by the sprinkles or jam.

3 Transfer the mixture to a shallow baking dish or loaf pan lined with plastic wrap and freeze until firm and frozen enough to scoop, at least 2 hours, depending on your freezer. Let sit at room temperature for 10 minutes or so before scooping* into a cup or a cone, topping with more sprinkles or whatever you like. (If you find it to be VERY frozen then you have a great freezer! Let it sit on the counter until scoopable.)

creamsicle

Before you get too excited, know that this is not an orange Popsicle with a cream center (the classic Creamsicle form), but more of a semifreddo-type situation that tastes just like a Creamsicle, historically one of my favorite flavor profiles. The texture is lighter and more fluffy than ice cream—thanks to whipped cream and, especially, to sweetened condensed milk, my absolute favorite modern culinary innovation. Here, it's providing sweetness and creamy texture, all while preventing this frozen treat from getting unscoopably hard (INSERT SCIENCE FACT HERE). Another nice thing about this dessert is that it can be served sliced while semifrozen (semifreddo!) or scooped once a bit firmer.

In a medium bowl with a whisk or an electric mixer, whip 3 cups of heavy cream to medium-stiff peaks. In a separate bowl, whisk together 1 14-ounce can sweetened condensed milk, ½ cup fresh lemon juice, ½ cup fresh orange juice, ¼ cup finely grated orange zest, and a nice pinch of salt. Gently fold the whipped cream into the sweetened condensed milk mixture.

Line a shallow baking dish or loaf pan with plastic wrap with a bit of overhang. Freeze the mixture in the prepared pan until firm and frozen, at least 2 hours, depending on your freezer. Let it sit at room temperature for 10 minutes or so before scooping into small bowls, or removing from the loaf pan and slicing like a loaf cake. Serve with more citrus on the side.

sundae

Remember when you were a kid and you thought, "When I'm an adult, I'll eat ice cream every night for dinner"? Well, wake up, that's a terrible idea. That said, I don't know a better way to end a dinner party than to continue the party in the form of a DIY Sundae Bar. The process can be messy and intimate, two very nice things in the right company. While it may seem like setting out containers of store-bought ice cream with store-bought sprinkles is phoning it in, it's in the homemade toppings and curation of cute small bowls and tiny spoons where your skills as host can really shine. So you're not a baker, that's fine. The Sundae Bar isn't really about baking. It's about showing people you care enough to think of all the toppings, and maybe even figure out how to make chocolate sauce from scratch and whip cream by hand.

While I believe in one's right to eat any number of ice cream flavors paired with any number of toppings, I am a purist, inviting only neutral flavors to my Sundae Bars. Vanilla. Caramel. Coffee. Chocolate. It's within the austerity of the neutral base that the flavored and textured toppings can truly shine. I'm sorry to be so basic, but, it's tough to beat the subtle flavor and bombastic joy of a scoop of vanilla ice cream showered with rainbow sprinkles. I'm sure you'll figure out what toppings speak to you, but here are my favorites to have on hand for these very special nights:

The Sauce: classic salty Caramel for All Occasions (page 288), creamy Tahini Caramel (page 289), A Very Good Chocolate Sauce (page 284). All warmed but not hot. Closer to room temperature, really. Too hot and the ice cream melts too quickly, and we hate that.

Sprinkles: Rainbow and store-bought.

Cherries, two types: Maraschino with the stems (the stem makes a difference, aesthetically) and the expensive Luxardo cherries (deeper cherry flavor, with good syrup for drizzling, too).

Cookies: Preferably very "regular" ones like Oreos, Nabisco chocolate wafers, or graham crackers. Crumble them into bowls to top your ice cream.

Bananas Foster-ish Bananas (page 210) are unparalleled in creating an impossibly sloppy, delicious version of a banana split.

Whipped cream (page 278) or **50/50** (page 279), and lots of it.

Aside from any combination of the above, the only other pieces of advice I have to give are: Have at least two containers of each ice cream flavor, keeping one in the freezer, so you can switch them out when they get too soft. Set out all your small and medium bowls and spoons—you'll need them. Don't do this on a white rug, especially a shag one where the sprinkles will grind into the fibers, forever becoming a part of your home.

Indulge in a Sundae Bar once and you'll be reminded why, exactly, you don't eat ice cream every night (adult onset lactose intolerance, anyone?), but for one night, it sure is a magical way to spend your time.

mint and chip
ice cream cake

Makes one tall 9-inch cake

9-inch disc of chocolate cake
(you can cut this out of the
All-Purpose Chocolate Sheet
Cake, page 112)

2 quarts mint chip ice cream
(or whatever flavor you like!)

2 cups/460g heavy cream

¼ cup/30g powdered sugar

Pinch of salt

Do ahead
The quintessential do-ahead, ice
cream cake can be assembled
1 week ahead, tightly wrapped in
plastic, and frozen.

Ice cream cake, as the name implies, is ice cream, shaped and frosted like a cake. Ideally, there is also actual cake or some sort of cookie crust, to prevent leaking and give your ice cream something to melt into. And you can (and should) frost it with sweetened whipped cream (rather than buttercream, which isn't all that delicious once frozen).

While technically "any ice cream can be made into an ice cream cake," I wouldn't know because aside from regular vanilla, mint and chip is the only ice cream I eat. Thrifty's made the best until they got bought by Rite Aid and now they don't sell ice cream like they used to. Now, my preferred brand is Baskin-Robbins (I'm a legacy brand girl, what can I say). The reason isn't because they use the highest-quality dairy and most fair trade chocolate—I'm not sure they do!–it's because it's not too sweet, the chocolate is in flecked form, not chunk- or hunk-size, and the ratio of chocolate to ice cream is extremely good. And sue me, I like the fake mint flavor. Fresh mint leaves steeped in hot dairy will never, ever give you something that tastes as good as mint extract or artificial mint flavor. I hate to say it, you hate to read it, we all know it's true.

1   Line a 9-inch springform pan with plastic wrap, making sure there's some plastic wrap hanging over the edges. Place the cake round on the bottom.

2   Let the ice cream soften on your counter for 10 minutes or so—you want the texture to be slightly softer than simply "scoopable" but decidedly not "melted." Spoon the ice cream out onto the cake and place a piece of plastic wrap directly on top. Use your palms to smush the ice cream down, making sure it's in one even layer. (You could use a spoon, but using your hands is faster and honestly more fun.) Place it in the freezer while you make the whipped cream.

3   In a large bowl with a whisk, an electric hand mixer, or whatever you want, beat the heavy cream to medium peaks, then whisk in the powdered sugar. It might feel a touch sweeter than your average whipped cream, but that's because it's getting frozen, which dulls flavors, including sweetness. Beat until you've got nice, pillowy stiff peaks and whisk in a nice pinch of salt, for seasoning.

4 Remove the cake from the freezer and peel back the plastic wrap. Still inside the springform, spoon about 1 cup of the whipped cream on top of the ice cream and "frost" the top of the cake, just to create a nice even layer of whipped cream, then pop it back into the freezer for at least 2 hours. Keep the rest of the whipped cream refrigerated.

5 When you're ready to serve, carefully unmold the ice cream cake—if it still feels a little too mushy/malleable for your liking, pop it back into the freezer until it feels solid enough to exist without its frame.

6 Once the cake is frozen and ready, remove the springform sides and frost the outside and the top with the remaining whipped cream. This can be put back into the freezer, if you like, or sliced and served as is. I find larger, fatter slices to be more dramatic, but they are perhaps too much for one person, so feel free to encourage sharing.

Other combinations

You shouldn't have to dig too deep to find the ice cream cake combination of your dreams. First, know that either sheet cake in this book (pages 108 and 112) would make a great base layer. And, second, if mint and chip simply aren't an option, here is what I'd choose:

Yellow cake with sprinkles added + **vanilla ice cream**
Cover with whipped cream and sprinkles, of course. On The Approval Matrix, this is lowbrow brilliant and undeniably perfect in its basicness.

Chocolate cake + **caramel ice cream**
Everyone makes caramel ice cream now, so don't worry. This would be good topped with chopped nuts, reminding me of a candy bar. Alternatively, just eat a frozen candy bar?

Yellow cake + **strawberry ice cream**
It's not strawberry shortcake, but it's close. Garnish with fresh strawberries, leaving some of the green tops on for fun.

i've got all this fruit, now what?

If it were up to me, this whole book would really be called "I've Got All This Fruit, Now What?" but I'll settle for a chapter. Fruit is the reason you're reading this book. I like dessert because there is fruit involved and part of why I like fruit is because I can turn it into dessert. Fruit: nature's candy. Cheesy sentiment but true. It comes sweetened, acidic, juicy—all the things that make dessert worth craving.

When in season, ripe and perfect, it doesn't need anything other than itself to present as dessert. In many places in the world, that's the case: The meal ends and out comes a gorgeous platter of fruit, sliced just so, perfectly peeled, gloriously nude. I think this is a perfect dessert and if after reading this book, that's all you have the bandwidth for, I support you. But there is more to it than that, if you'd like.

While I proclaim this to be the dessert book for those who don't bake, the recipes that follow in this chapter are really, truly, and deeply desserts for people who don't bake. There are recipes for those who like to follow recipes, but there are also ideas, suggestions, and vague concepts that will turn almost any fruit into dessert. Sometimes it's simply dairy (or a dairy substitute) plus fruit, an undeniable classic. Sometimes it's poaching, roasting, or simmering the fruit with a bit of sugar or honey to coax out the sugars hiding within. It can be many things, but I promise that if baking makes you nervous, this chapter can be your safe space.

bananas foster-ish bananas

Serves 4-6

4-5 bananas, halved lengthwise

½ cup/105g light or dark brown sugar

½ cup/120g light or dark rum or bourbon

2 tablespoons/1 ounce/30g unsalted butter

1 vanilla bean or cinnamon stick (optional)

2-3 star anise seed pods (optional)

½ cup/75g almonds, walnuts, or hazelnuts (optional), toasted and coarsely chopped

Vanilla ice cream, for serving

Flaky sea salt, for sprinkling

Do ahead
Bananas can be Foster'd a few hours in advance. Rewarm gently in the oven before serving (they really are so good warm).

I do love the idea of dousing desserts in alcohol and lighting them on fire. For the effect, for the show, for the DRAMA. But, to quote myself, "yeah, I'm not gonna do that." And I don't think you should do that, either! Even the waiters at my beloved Keens Steakhouse stopped doing it tableside as it proved to be a danger to all involved. Let's practice safe Bananas Foster, shall we?

To do so, simply roast the bananas and booze at a high temperature, to keep the shape of the bananas intact and create a thick, glossy sauce made from dark rum, brown sugar, and the spices of your choosing (vanilla beans, star anise, and cinnamon sticks are all appropriate). Serve these bananas and their delicious caramel-y nuts over a bowl of vanilla ice cream. You'll be so glad you did.

1   Preheat the oven to 425°F.

2   Place the bananas in a shallow baking dish (a shallow pot would also work; a cast-iron skillet is okay here, too) and cover with the sugar, rum, butter, and any spices or "aromatics" you are feeling in the moment.

3   Roast until the sugar has caramelized and the bananas are nicely translucent and impossibly tender, 35–40 minutes (depending on the ripeness of the bananas, really).

4   Remove the pan from the oven and add the toasted nuts (if using) to the sticky banana caramel sauce, stirring to coat.

5   Serve the bananas and sticky nuts over a bowl of vanilla ice cream, sprinkled with flaky salt.

Bourbon, whiskey, rye—I can't really tell the difference between any of them, but know they're all fair game here if you don't have rum on hand. Regarding the spices, you could use ground, but I find the whole star anise, cinnamon sticks, cloves, whatever, to be more subtle on the tongue and stunning to the eyes. Everyone wins, especially your bananas.

how to

How to tell your fruit is ripe. Most of the time, the ripeness of the fruit is decided by farmers and workers who dutifully choose the ripest-but-not-so-ripe-it-turns-to-mush fruit to be transported to small regional farmers' markets or big box grocery stores. But there are still ways that we, the consumers, can make further selections to the best of our ability, and honestly I find the whole process of determining ripeness to be very sensual. Or at least, it should be. SMELL. Press firmly on the skin of an apple or musk melon (cantaloupe especially, and especially the navel-looking button where the vine once was) and at their ripest, they'll smell like those apple- or melon-flavored Japanese gummies. At their best, perfectly ripe pears, peaches, raspberries, and strawberries can be detected from the next room over by simply existing at room temperature. FEEL. Raspberries can barely be held between two fingers without spilling their juices. Stone fruit has a certain give, going from firm to supple. The best way to test one is to use the side of your thumb to gently press on the top, right next to the stem. It should feel almost like the space between your index finger and thumb when making a fist (not unlike medium-rare steak, if you can bear the comparison). Figs are like this, too. I've heard a watermelon should feel dense, as in the heavier it is, the juicer it is inside. LOOK. Things you can tell just by looking at (fruit): When a blackberry is ripe, each small orb appears so dark it's almost black, and it's plump and full of juice. Rhubarb turns bright pink. Bananas develop deep brown spots on the peel. Strawberries turn ruby red with little to no white top beneath the stem. EAT. Does the juice dribble down your forearm? Did you stain an article of clothing but, too distracted by how good the fruit tastes, cease to care? Does the fruit taste like a cartoon version of the fruit or "remind you of flavored ChapStick"? Does eating the fruit make you want to never eat another one of that fruit again because that sort of perfection is unlikely to ever happen again? Your fruit is ripe.

hard-roasted pears

Serves 6-8

2 pounds/910g pears or apples, halved lengthwise, peeled and/or cored if you like

1½ cups/355g white wine

½ cup/110g granulated sugar

¼ cup/60g molasses or ¼ cup/50g light brown sugar

2 tablespoons/1 ounce/30g unsalted butter, cut into small pieces (optional)

For the optional aromatics

Vanilla seeds, from a scraped vanilla bean

A few slices of fresh ginger

Fresh herbs, such as thyme, rosemary, or lemon verbena

Citrus zest

Spices, such as star anise or cinnamon sticks

Eat with
Creamy blue cheese, Chocolate-Sour Cream Pound Cake (page 133) and crème fraîche, or Hot Buttered Rum Pudding (page 150).

Do ahead
Pears can be roasted a few hours before you want to serve them. Leftovers can be stored in the fridge, but are at their best the evening they're made.

Roasted fruit of any sort is generally a good idea, but some fruits turn to mush, which isn't really what I'm after (unless, of course, I am: See Oven Jam, page 239). Pears (and apples), however, when roasted become simultaneously tender AND hold their shape—a true miracle. They also take kindly to assertive flavors, which is why you'll often find them cooked with alcohol like brandy or red wine. Here, I've used white wine for the acidity and a little molasses for the gorgeous color and "adult" flavor.

I like to serve these at the end of a very long, robust meal, after the plates have been cleared and it's not clear if there's even room for dessert at all. And, if there is, maybe it's just a modest bowl of good ice cream (vanilla, pistachio, or caramel) next to some hard-roasted pears, with some excellent Concord grapes for snacking on in between sips of very adult-tasting amaro. Or, if your idea of dessert means nice cheeses, then these would be right at home with a soft-ripened cow's milk cheese, or deeply veiny blue cheese.

I never peel my pears and I don't really mind the core, especially if the pears are small. But as always, feel free to peel if you must, and if you're looking for a good way to remove the core and for some reason don't own a melon baller (who among us), I like to use a 1-teaspoon measuring spoon to scoop it out.

1   Preheat the oven to 425°F. Place the pears cut-side down in a shallow baking dish (a shallow pot would work; but avoid using cast-iron) and cover with the wine, sugar, molasses, butter (if using), and any aromatics you are feeling in the moment.

2   Roast the pears until the wine is reduced almost completely and the pears are impossibly tender, 1 hour to 1 hour 10 minutes (depending on the variety of pear, really).

fruit salad

When I hear "fruit salad," I think of two things. One is the first dessert I fell in love with that I, still to this day, have never eaten: the Gargouillou from Michel Bras. A riff on his famous vegetable dish of the same name, it's a symphony of fruits, plated like they all just fell on the forest floor. Each fruit is cooked or treated with delicate care, a soft touch, receiving its own special treatment to bring out its maximum potential. Then, there's the version of fruit salad that's basically a bowl of whole grapes, cubed melon, and the occasional rogue berry or sliced kiwi left to marinate on a conference table. My fruit salad is neither of those things, but something simpler than the former, more interesting than the latter.

To me, a fruit salad is a salad made of fruit. It can be savory, but for our purposes here (a dessert book), it will be sweet. It will not be overthought, but it will be considered. On the following pages are some do's and don'ts that will help you make a successful fruit salad.

Do season your salad. Yes, with (flaky) salt and (coarsely ground black) pepper, but also with sweetness (honey, maple syrup) and acidity (fresh citrus juice). Spiciness is welcomed (crushed red pepper flakes, Aleppo chile flakes, or gochugaru are my favorites) as are herbs (mint, lavender) and spices (crushed fennel seed, sumac). Don't use regular grapes—they're rarely remarkable. Do use Concord grapes—they're always spectacular. Don't feel pressured to have all colors of the rainbow represented. Do embrace monochromatic combinations of fruits. Gold on gold, purple on purple, red on red. Chic, simple, gorgeous. Don't cut all your fruits into small, uniform cubes. Boring to look at, boring to eat. Do cut your fruits into interesting shapes and different sizes. Visual texture counts for a lot in a fruit salad.

The nice thing about dessert is that it doesn't have to be a production; the offer itself can be enough. A little sweet something. A square of chocolate. A bowl of tangerines. A tiny cup of crushed raspberries swirled into thick sour cream.

This "recipe" (it's not really a recipe) might be the best illustration of what I mean by being a dessert for people who don't bake. It's also for people who don't cook, who may have never cooked, who have never thought of cooking. That said, it's also a dessert for people who love dessert, who make dessert every chance they get, who could never imagine a meal without dessert. It's truly for everyone, and the short ingredient list belies how transcendent the combination truly is. To me, this dessert is extremely romantic, sexy, sultry in the way that its casualness gives way to something very desirable, almost by accident. That's hot.

Enhanced with just the smallest amount of sugar to encourage the juices to flow forth, raspberries really are the full package for this: tart, juicy, textured with seeds in a way that is welcomed and delightful. But a similar energy could be achieved with any fruit that speaks to you at the moment, raw, roasted, whatever you like: crushed peaches seasoned with a bit of lime juice, a spoonful of tart apricot jam (see page 236), or bits of Slow-Roasted Rhubarb (page 233) are all good ideas to get your mind racing.

Serve in the summer, after a wine-drunk lunch on a blanket or after midnight at a late-night Saturday dinner party. It's a true all-occasion, any-season delight (the sugar added allows you to get away with less-than-naturally-exquisite fruit, another reason this dessert is perfect and practical).

Put some **raspberries** in a bowl and sprinkle them with just a little bit of **sugar,** a light dusting (you can always add more if they need it, but I doubt they do). Use a fork and smash them—not until they're an unrecognizable mash, just gently broken down and crushed. Wait a few minutes to release their juicy potential.

Spoon a little bit of **sour cream** (unsweetened) into a serving cup, mug, or bowl. Top with a little bit of the crushed raspberries. Repeat this one or two more times, depending on how large your vessel is. You can swirl this together after it's been layered, or leave it parfait-style.

raspberries and sour cream

ice cream in melon

Eating ice cream from a seeded melon half, drizzled with honey, is an experience every living human should have at least one time in their life. Here, I am talking about melons in the muskmelon family, which include cantaloupe, canary melon, and honeydew—save your watermelon for something else like fruit salad (see page 218) or Frozen Melon with Crushed Berries (page 191).

To make, halve a **very ripe small-to-medium melon*** horizontally. Using a spoon, scoop out the seeds and goopy innards that surround the seeds. Fill the hole in the melon with **ice cream** (I am partial to vanilla here) and drizzle the top with **honey**. Give a sprinkle of **flaky salt** if it's available.

Resist the urge to put anything crunchy on top and just relish the beauty that is soft and creamy on top of soft and juicy. One of the reasons this works so well is that the melon truly holds the ice cream. I mean that in the literal sense— the melon serves as a perfectly functional little bowl to hold all sorts of things. Wine jelly, port, vanilla ice cream. But I also mean it in a figurative sense—a good, ripe melon is soft, floral, and sweet. Three gorgeous adjectives. The melon simply holds the ice cream in a gentle way, letting it be its luscious, milky self. A beautiful and underrepresented pairing, a perfect dessert.

*While it would change the name of the dessert entirely, I would be remiss not to mention this is also perfect done in a slightly scooped out perfectly ripe Hachiya persimmon, which to me has always had delightful melon-esque qualities.

naked peaches (and a casual trifle)

I think it's nice to take special care of fruit, and I do. In fact, I take care of my fruit in a way that I rarely take care of my vegetables. Maybe because I think of vegetables as sturdy, growing in the ground, yanked from vines, and tossed around in bags and boxes with a roughness that would simply not do for a berry or apricot. Fruit is inherently more delicate and needs more tenderness. I have had vegetables survive days at the bottom of my purse, the footwell of my car, and the back of my fridge, good as new, ready to be seared, roasted, fermented. Conversely, if I don't immediately transfer my raspberries to a satin-lined tray where none of them touch in an arid, draft-free environment, they are immediately ruined. Nectarines, if not given first-class transport on a feather-filled cushion, will certainly bruise, perhaps even suffer a puncture wound.

In the restaurants I've worked at, we'd bring berries back from the finest farms in California. Transported in tiny neon-green baskets nestled inside cardboard boxes, they always rode on somebody's lap to ensure minimal disruption. Once inside the kitchen, there was a full-on triage situation, delicately tumbling each basket of berries onto a parchment-lined full-sheet pan, gingerly spreading them apart because when they touch, they bruise, and if they bruise, they express their juice, and when there is juice, there is mold, and mold is death (to a berry).

While my fruit neurosis has mellowed, I sort of attach the same tenderness to preparing as I do storing. I'd never be caught dead peeling a carrot, but give me the hottest day of the year and there I'll be, dunking fresh peaches into boiling water to free them from the tyranny of their skins.

Sure, it's an unnecessary step for most things involving peaches: pies, galettes, jam. But sometimes when they are at their ripest and most perfect, there's the desire to get even closer to the fruit, removing even the suggestion of a barrier between you and the juicy flesh. When peeling, the point isn't so much for a more tender peach, only a more naked one, and that is the sexiest thing I could possibly imagine.

I am not here to get into the science behind it (because I don't know the science behind it), but I do know that when you use a knife to score a small, shallow "X" onto the bum of a peach, and dunk it for 30 seconds into a pot of boiling water, the skin will effortlessly free itself from the fruit . . . nothing short of a miracle.

All you have to do from there is use a bit of pressure from your thumb and forefinger to encourage the skin to slip off, revealing an extremely pleasingly slippery, very wet, and unclothed peach.

The best use of these peaches in my opinion is something where you can enjoy the silkiness of peach with absolutely no resistance, no skin to break through, only clear access to all its juice. A thought: a casual trifle. The name suggests casualness, and so here, I will deliver, with no measurements because I promise, you don't need them:

Layer your **freshly nude peaches** with creamy, cooled **vanilla pudding** (page 158) and thick slabs of **shortcake** (page 94) broken up into irregular pieces (like very large croutons) in your largest, flashiest serving bowl (I own one large clear bowl for precisely this purpose). Once inside the magic of the bowl, the shortcakes are softened by the juices of the peach and custardiness of the pudding, giving you exactly three separate but harmonious textures: crumbly, creamy, and juicy. Truly a remarkably refined experience, one best suited for a perfectly naked peach.*

*Truthfully, also wonderful with halved strawberries.

Disclaimer: I have before encountered peaches that refuse to be peeled, and I'm sad to say you can't force it. Not more time in the boiling water, not more force with your hands. You have to accept those peaches for who they are. You'll never know by looking at them, which is cruel, but peaches keep us guessing and I'd be lying if I said that's not part of their appeal.

This fruit cocktail isn't about drowning your fruit in syrup and hoping for a slightly better version of what comes in those little plastic cups. Here, it's about enjoying juicy fruit in a bowl with "a little something special" (alcohol). More commitment than simply an after-dinner drink, less work than making a dessert. To make a fruit cocktail you only have to have fruit and alcohol. This can be interpreted many ways, but for me, the best alcohol for a fruit cocktail is something lower proof, with a bit of sweetness, and something else it brings to the table, like herbaceousness, bitterness, or fruitiness. The best fruit to use here is something that's in season, preferably something juicy and soft rather than crunchy and hard. As is customary with fruit cocktail, you should feel comfortable mixing and matching as many fruits as your maximalist heart desires, but as a general rule I'd recommend no fewer than two, no more than five. Figs and pear + a sweet amaro, such as Montenegro, Furlani, or Nonino / Plums, sour cherries, and blackberries + cassis / Peaches, apricots, and oranges + Lillet (red or white) / Blackberries, raspberries, and sweet cherries + red vermouth. To make a fruit cocktail, first prepare the fruit. If you're using something larger than a berry, say a plum, fig, or apricot, slice the fruit to expose the interior (it will absorb the alcohol better). Then, place the fruit in a bowl, preferably something shallow. Drizzle the fruit with enough liquor to see it pool at the bottom of the bowl, then let it sit, or not. It's as delicious the moment it's made as it is the next day. If you're serving this outside on an especially warm day, scatter the fruit with some ice to chill it down.

rhubarb

slow-roasted rhubarb

Its presence is fleeting, appearing sporadically in particular climates for only a few weeks in the spring. Raw, it has a crunchy, celery-esque texture and unforgivable sourness. But roasted with a bit of sugar, it transforms into a fruit that's jammy and tender, with a stringy silkiness almost like the inside of a long roasted eggplant, with an incredible balance of sweet and sour. I wish it were more popular and therefore, more accessible, but unless it's growing wild in your yard (looking at you, residents of the northeastern part of the USA), the lack of broad availability makes it a challenge. But I'm telling you: If you see it, get excited.

is a gift

While I am of course a fan of baking it into a cake (using it instead of figs on page 121 and instead of stone fruit on page 129) and in galettes (pages 36–39), a more simple and low-stakes way to test the rhubarb waters is to scatter stalks that have been halved lengthwise with a generous amount of sugar and slow-roast it in a 300°F oven for about 1½ hours, where the juices flow forth from the fruit, reduce, and caramelize around the stalks and create a deliciously tart sticky sauce all on its own. Rhubarb prepared this way is good to eat alongside creamy desserts like the Tangy Buttermilk Pie (page 56), Milk and Honey Semolina Pudding (page 161), Toasted Rice Pudding (page 164), or a giant bowl of vanilla ice cream. If I were a pavlova person (I'm not), I would say this would be great there, too, and if you have a copy of my last cookbook, *Nothing Fancy*, know that the panna cotta recipe in there is begging to spend time with this rhubarb.

berries in cream

Crushed raspberries in sour cream (see page 222) is truly one of my favorite things to make and is as simple as it sounds . . . but this is the original "thrown together" something something. Well suited to follow lunch or an early dinner (my favorite kind of dinner), this is a real whisper of a dessert, eating berries the way you'd enjoy cereal. It's fun, it's casual, it says "I care, but I'm also busy. I care, but I'm also full. I care, but I want to go swimming after this."

To do this, all you need is a bowl of **good berries**— a mix is always nice, **strawberries** are my favorite. Halve or quarter them if large, leaving any **blueberries** whole. To do this with "just okay" fruit will yield "just okay" results (save the "just okay" fruit for jam, where it's cooked and sweetened to achieve "very good" results).

Place the berries in a bowl—and drizzle with good **heavy cream**. Not whipped, not sweetened. Tasting dairy in its full element reminds you that it really should be something enjoyed sparingly, as it is truly special. Decadent and milky, naturally thick and luscious, needing nothing more than a little fruit in between spoonfuls. Eating this with a nice spoon makes me feel simultaneously childish and impossibly elegant—exactly where you want to be when you're eating dessert.

so you want to make jam

My best advice for anyone wanting to make jam for the first time, or for the millionth time, is to accept (and appreciate!) that each batch will likely be different from the last. Blueberries from Maine have different levels of acidity than the ones from California, peaches appearing in August are juicer, sweeter, and softer than the ones out in June. The variety in fruit either from season or locale means you may need a little less sugar from one batch to the next, more lemon juice here and there, occasionally a longer cook time to properly break down and thicken.

For me, this inconsistency is all part of the joy of making jam, which can be either a scientific or intuitive process, depending on the type of person you are (I am definitely the latter). Like all of us, jam contains multitudes. It wants to be adjusted, listened to, and paid attention to. Go into your jam making with a heightened sense of awareness, tasting the fruit, prepared to adjust, to pivot, to doctor with whatever it may need to allow it to become the best, most balanced, fruitiest jam you've ever had.

stovetop jam

4 pounds/1.8kg blueberries, raspberries, or blackberries; or 4½ pounds/2kg strawberries (hulled and quartered), peaches, nectarines, plums, or apricots (pitted and chopped)

3 cups/660g sugar

¼ cup/60g fresh lemon or lime juice (about 2 lemons or limes)

Eat with
Toast with lots of butter and salt, over ice cream, swirled into cake batter (see page 118).

Do ahead
The jam can be made 2–3 months ahead and stored in the refrigerator.

Note
As the jam cooks, the liquid reduces, the sugars thicken, and the natural pectins activate. You'll notice the liquid go from a rapid, rolling boil with smaller bubbles to a slow, thick, tar-like boil with larger bubbles. This is the stage at which it's most important to stir constantly along the bottom of the pot to prevent the fruit from burning.

While jam often feels like sugar thickened with fruit, this here is a celebration of the fruit itself, cooked just long enough to get rid of excess moisture with just enough sugar to highlight its texture and flavor.

While I do enjoy a low-sugar jam, it's not quite as good a candidate for canning. (The sugar in jam acts as a preservative.) That said, "not canning" has never once stopped me from making jam; I just got into the habit of keeping it in the fridge instead of the pantry.

1   In a large heavy-bottomed pot, toss the fruit and sugar together. Let sit at least 15 minutes, up to overnight, tossing periodically to dissolve the sugar (this will help coax the juices out of the fruit to give the jam a head start).

2   Bring the fruit to a strong simmer over medium-high heat, until the juices start to boil, 3–4 minutes.

3   Reduce the heat to medium and continue cooking. Using a wooden spoon or spatula, stir the jam occasionally at first, then more frequently as the jam cooks and juices thicken (see Note). Cook until most of the liquid has evaporated and the fruit has started to break down to the point you'd start to call it "jammy," 40–50 minutes. How much it breaks down will depend on the fruit (e.g., strawberries and peaches are likely to remain chunkier while raspberries and apricots will break down almost entirely).

4   Add the lemon juice and continue to cook, stirring constantly, until the jam has returned to its previously thickened state, another 8–10 minutes. Test the jam by spooning a bit of jam onto a plate and pop it into the fridge for a few minutes, then drag your finger through it—it should hold its shape without appearing watery or runny. If it's not there yet, cook a few minutes more. (Some fruit, like strawberries, contain more water and less natural pectin than, say, a raspberry. So the jam may never be quite as thick or gelled, but will nevertheless be delicious.)

5   Remove from the heat. Using a ladle (carefully! The jam is very hot!), divide jam among 4 half-pint/250ml jars and seal immediately. Let come to room temperature on your counter before refrigerating (or canning).

oven jam

*Makes about 4 cups/1 liter or
4 half-pint/250ml jars*

4–5 pounds/1.8kg–2.3kg stone
fruit, pitted

2 cups/440g sugar

¼ cup/60g fresh lemon, lime,
or orange juice (or water*)

Aromatics (optional)**

*Water would work, in a pinch—
you just want to start roasting
the fruit with a bit of liquid in the
bottom to prevent the sugar
from caramelizing.

**You could, of course, include
some sort of aromatic here, like
a split vanilla bean, a hearty herb
you're fond of, or some citrus
zest—but it can be sticky to fish
out after, so I typically save that
sort of thing for hard-roasted
fruit (see Hard-Roasted Pears,
page 217).

Making jam on your countertop requires a not-insignificant amount
of babysitting. There is also the splattering, the potential scorching . . .
Listen, I love it, but even I have thought: "There's got to be a better way."
And sometimes, there isn't. Sometimes, with fruits like tiny berries,
the only way to fill a multitude of mason jars with ruby red raspberry
jam is to do it in a large pot over medium heat for what feels like an
eternity, wearing a long-sleeved shirt you don't mind splattering.

But sometimes, there *is* a better way. Sometimes . . . there is oven jam.

Best suited for larger fruits that hold their shape as they roast,
like peaches, plums, and apricots (and for when you have lots of time
on your hands), oven jam is almost real jam, but different. Done in
the oven (as advertised) rather than the stovetop, you are effectively
slow-roasting the fruit in a pool of concentrated, syrupy juices to
spoon over ice cream, spread onto toast, or fold into cake batter.
It's chunkier and coarser than classic jam, requiring less sugar than
the conventional method. Store in the refrigerator for a few weeks
to use as you please, extending the season of whatever fruit you're
excited about for just a little bit longer.

1   Preheat the oven to 325°F.

2   Place the fruit in a 3-quart (3-liter) baking dish (a standard 9 × 13-inch
    baking dish) and toss with the sugar and lemon juice. Roast, stirring as
    often as you feel, until the fruit begins to succumb to the heat of the oven.
    Toward the end, it can be helpful to give the fruit an encouraging squash
    with a wooden spoon or spatula, but typically it will just fall apart naturally.
    This should take, on average, about 2 hours, but will depend largely on
    the fruit you're using. If it looks like the liquid is still too syrupy, keep
    roasting until it's properly thickened, with large, slow bubbles. Feel free to
    adjust post-oven with more acidity if you like, before storing in the fridge.

3   To store, spoon the oven jam into mason jars or plastic containers.
    Seal and refrigerate. This jam is not meant to be shelf-stable—think of it
    more as a fridge jam. It will last at least 1 month, probably longer—you'll
    know to get rid of it when the taste changes or if mold starts to grow.

Marmalade, let it be known, takes forever to make.
There's the slicing of the citrus fruit, for which there are no shortcuts, then an optional—but recommended—24-hour soaking period before you even start cooking. Then the fruit gets boiled for at least 1½ hours before you add sugar, at which point it cooks for another 45 minutes, at least. Then there's the intense babysitting of the pot as the marmalade gets close, with you being careful to stir to prevent the sugars from caramelizing or scorching. Once all that's ready, you're dealing with the painstakingly careful distribution of hot marmalade into sterilized jars and the whole canning process (if you're canning). Then you're spending more time than you'd like cleaning up the sticky bits of fruit and sugar that ended up all over your clothes, your forearms, and the walls of your kitchen. It's a full day and a half of your life.

On top of it being time-consuming, making marmalade can be unpredictable and a little bit fussy. Each batch is delightfully yet annoyingly unique, depending on the acidity, sweetness, and pectin content of your particular citrus, the size of your pot, the ferocity of your boil. It's never exact and there are no two batches that behave just the same. Also, I regret to inform you: You will almost certainly burn yourself on the spits and spurts of hot, syrupy citrus juice as the marmalade enters its final stages of cooking, causing you to wonder if the marmalade is, in fact, trying to kill you.

But damn, spread that gloriously golden jellified citrus onto thick, nearly burnt toast with a smear of salted butter, sprinkled with more bits of flaky salt and maybe even some pepper because it's good that way, and you feel so refined and elegant that you forget everything. Spoon the marmalade on top of vanilla ice cream or stir it into something else rich and creamy, like ricotta or full-fat Greek yogurt. As you dip your spoon into it for the eighth time, think: "Wow, I can't believe I made something so wonderful. Was this really so much work? I can't wait to do it again." You forget it all. How much damn time it took, how annoying it was, how it almost tried to kill you.

Marmalade, I love you, you're worth it.

marmalade, i love you

whole citrus marmalade

*Makes about 4 cups/1 liter; four
half-pint/250ml jars*

3 pounds/1.35kg citrus*

2½ cups/550g demerara sugar**

2½ cups/550g granulated sugar

¼ cup/60g fresh lemon juice
(about 2 lemons)

*My favorite batch used a mix
of pink grapefruit, tangerines,
oranges, lemons, and 2 small
kumquats (which did nothing
but delighted me to include all
the same).

**As I learned from *The River
Cottage Preserves Handbook*,
replacing half the sugar with
demerara sugar really does
provide a special something
here for oranges, giving a sort
of caramelized flavor and
gorgeous sunset color. If the
batch is predominantly oranges/
tangerines and the like, I highly
recommend using it. For things
like grapefruit or lemon, I think all
regular sugar is the right move.

Eat with
Toast with lots of butter and salt,
over ice cream, swirled into cake
batter (page 118).

Do ahead
Marmalade can be made at least
3 months ahead and stored in
the refrigerator.

**Marmalade is everything all at once—chunky bits of bitter peel
existing amongst a glorious, sweet jelly. It's my favorite of all the jams
and jellies in the world, a thing I look forward to making every year.
If you live in a place that has access to a wide variety of citrus, exotic
or exotic-to-you (New York is sadly not that place!), this is the time to
experiment. If you don't, mail-order citrus is a thing, and I will throw
my money at any and all mail-order fruit come citrus season!**

1 Using a sharp knife, slice the peel, including the pith (the white part),
away from the fruit of the citrus, just like you're preparing the citrus
for a salad.

2 Cut the peels into slivers. This thickness is a personal preference, but I like
to do about ⅛ inch. You could do even thinner, or go slightly thicker if you
like. Soak these slivers in water for 24 hours, if you have the time—this will
make the next-day cooking process a bit quicker, giving the peels a good
head start (if not, go ahead and proceed with step 3).

3 Thinly slice the fruit, taking care to avoid slicing into any seeds and
discarding any seeds along the way.

4 Drain the soaked peels and transfer them to a large heavy-bottomed pot.
Cover with 10 cups/2.4 liters water. Bring to a boil, then reduce the heat to
medium-high and cook for 1–1½ hours at a strong-ish boil, until the water
has evaporated by about half and the peels are nearly translucent and
quite tender (the time here will depend greatly on the size and power of
your burner).

5 Add the sliced fruit and return the pot to a boil. Cook until the liquid is
reduced by about one-third, 20–25 minutes or so.

6 Add the sugar(s) and stir to make sure it's totally dissolved without settling
to the bottom (where it could caramelize, which we don't want). Cook
the sugar and fruit together until the contents of the pot stop boiling
and start bubbling (not a technical term, but I think of boiling as very fast,
and a bubble as slower and decidedly thicker), 40–45 minutes or so.
You may want to skim any egregiously foamy bubbles that have formed
and are now likely clinging to the sides of the pot—do it with a regular
spoon, just like you're skimming a stock or broth.

7   Things will happen quickly at this stage so pay attention here: As the liquid evaporates, the sugars start to reach a temperature that creates that telltale "set" (think making caramel or other sorts of confections that require you to cook sugar to a certain temperature). Stirring constantly keeps the temperature even throughout and prevents scorching or caramelization on the bottom of the pot, so stir, stir, keep stirring.

8   If you're using a thermometer, cook the marmalade to 220°F, then give it a "gel test" by spooning a bit of marmalade onto a plate and popping it into the fridge to see how it sets—it should be marmalade texture, which is to say, fruit set amongst a clear, jelly-ish liquid, not a syrup. If it needs more thickening, cook a few more minutes and try again. Thermometers aren't foolproof! If you don't have a thermometer, simply do the gel test. If you're really not sure if it's done or not or how much longer to cook it, here is what I will say: A too-thick marmalade ends up tasting like candy, so I always err on the side of cooking a little less rather than more (better texture, fresher citrus flavor, less sickly sweet). If the worst thing that happens is you've got a slightly runny marmalade, I would still consider that a win.

9   Once the marmalade is just about done cooking, add the lemon juice and continue to boil another 3–5 minutes, just to get the texture back to where it was before you added the lemon juice, then remove from the heat. Let it cool in the pot for a little bit (10 minutes or so) before dividing among half-pint/250ml jars or containers (this allows the liquid to cool and thicken ever so slightly, allowing the slices of citrus to be more evenly suspended/distributed). And please be careful, even slightly cooled marmalade is still extremely hot!

10 To store, I like to keep mine in the fridge for as long as it lasts. I can't quote you an exact life-span because I still have some from early 2020 (it's 2022 as I write this) that is still going strong, but as I'm sure you've gathered, I do not work for the FDA, so take that with a grain of salt.

I'll never quit going to therapy,
but cutting the peel away from pounds
of citrus, slicing it into thin strips,
and cooking them down with sugar
and water until you've achieved
marmalade status is a good proxy
on our off-days.

frozen fruit

My first real job as a sixteen-year-old was at a San Fernando outpost of Jamba Juice (store #28), which I only mention to say that I'm no stranger to the power of frozen fruit, whether or not it's going into a smoothie. Frankly, I love it, and find it highly valuable both as a purchased ingredient and as a preserving technique. Paradoxically, one of my greatest joys is going to a farm or farmers' market and buying too much of whatever impossibly ripe and ready-to-be-consumed fruit they have. It either gets eaten all within twenty-four hours, baked into something, turned into jam, or, before it's had a chance to age even a day, frozen in resealable bags.

Some might say that to freeze perfectly ripe fruit is a crime, but I say it's prudent. Have you ever known the joy of pulling a bag of peak-season strawberries from the freezer in the depths of February to then thaw and bake it into a cake or stew into a jam? It's the scent of another time, filling the air with hope and the promise that, no, it WON'T be frigid forever and, yes, the sun WILL shine again. It's bliss.

To give your peak, perfect fruit the best chance at success for another life several months down the road, prepare it as you would if you were going to use it immediately; i.e., pit your cherries, hull your strawberries, slice your peaches, peel your bananas. Doing the work now will give you something effortless when the time comes. Depending on the eventual application, they can be (1) frozen in 16-ounce bags for easy measuring—best for things like jam or pie filling, or (2) scattered on a sheet pan, frozen, and then stored—best if you're looking to do things like disperse the fruit evenly inside a cake batter or blend into smoothies.

morning times, snack times

This is admittedly a stretch—breakfast is not dessert, and dessert should not be eaten for breakfast. But there is enough crossover in the items you may eat for snacktime (in the morning or otherwise) that are sweet enough to count as dessert to rationalize their inclusion here, or at least that's what I argued to my editor. Regardless, I sort of see it as a little bit of a bonus chapter. Here you'll find things that might not find themselves at your table at the end of the night but rather at the beginning (or middle) of your day, things that are both savory and sweet, and things that toe the line (apologies in advance, but cornbread should be well seasoned and, yes, that means with some added sugar!), really earning their keep in a book titled Sweet Enough. The time of day they're served should make the recipes here no less worthy of celebration—if you stuck a birthday candle in those sticky cinnamon rolls (page 254) I would be thrilled—or earning a spot in your baking repertoire.

seedy breakfast cake

Makes one 9 × 4-inch loaf

Cooking spray, for the pan

1½ cups/220g all-purpose flour

2–3 tablespoons poppy seeds, plus more for sprinkling

2–3 tablespoons white sesame seeds, toasted, plus more for sprinkling

2 tablespoons flaxseeds (optional)

1 tablespoon/12g baking powder

2 teaspoons fennel seeds (optional)

1 teaspoon/4g kosher salt

½ cup/110g granulated sugar, plus more for dusting

¼ cup/50g light brown sugar

1 cup/180ml whole-milk Greek yogurt or full-fat sour cream, plus more (optional) for serving

2 large eggs

½ cup/115g neutral oil, such as grapeseed or canola

1–2 ripe bananas (optional), smashed with a fork

Eat with
Sliced citrus and yogurt, a cup of tea or coffee, your hands in the car.

Do ahead
This cake stays good for about 5 days, stored tightly wrapped at room temperature.

This is called Breakfast Cake because I find it to be the perfect thing to nibble on with your cup of PG Tips (or coffee, or whatever you're drinking in the morning), approximating "breakfast." It's not healthy (it's cake), but it does have an excellent granola energy to it that makes it seem like the only proper time to eat it is in the morning (I can speak from personal experience that it's also good to eat in the afternoon, for a picnic, on a hike, in the car at night when you are in traffic and skipped dinner, for dessert with ice cream, etc.).

By definition this cake should contain a lot of seeds, but you can mix and match based on availability. Additions are also encouraged, including but not limited to: a large handful of rolled oats or ½ cup chopped nuts or pumpkin seeds.

1   Preheat the oven to 350°F. Spray a 9 × 4-inch loaf pan with cooking spray and line the long sides with parchment (for easy removal).

2   In a medium bowl, whisk together the flour, poppy seeds, sesame seeds, flaxseeds (if using), baking powder, fennel seeds (if using), and salt.

3   In a large bowl, whisk together both sugars, the yogurt, eggs, and oil (now is when you'd add the banana, if using). Add the flour mixture and using the same whisk (or switch to a spatula), gently mix until you don't have any visible dry spots or lumps, taking care not to overmix the batter.

4   Transfer the batter to the prepared loaf pan and sprinkle with a bit more poppy seeds and sesame seeds, followed by a good dusting of granulated sugar.

5   Bake the cake until it's puffed, golden, and springs back when pressed on the surface and the sides visibly pull away from the sides of the pan, 1 hour 5 minutes to 1 hour 15 minutes (on the longer side if you've added a banana—loaf cakes take a long time!).

6   Let cool completely before slicing.

cinnamon rolls

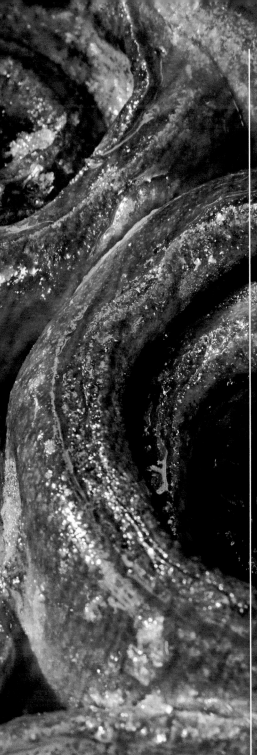

The cinnamon roll is a dessert, it's breakfast, it's in the breakfast chapter of a dessert book. A generous smear of butter, brown sugar, and cinnamon on the dough is great for an internal swirl of sweetness and the iconic peel-apart journey it takes you on. By all accounts, that should be "enough," but somewhere along the way we decided to either frost them like a cake (why) or drizzle them with a flavorless, milky-white substance that has never done anything for me, visually or otherwise. But I get it, our human lizard brains are programmed to enjoy SHINY, GLAZED things and FROSTED things, and when cinnamon rolls come out of the oven, regardless of what's going on inside of them, they look dry.

At the risk of sounding arrogant, I feel I've come to a better cinnamon roll conclusion by applying some sticky bun logic. Adding maple syrup to the bottom of the pan for the rolls to bake into, then brushing them with maple syrup on top immediately out of the oven (not unlike a babka), gives you something between glazed-but-not-wet and sticky-in-a-good-way. The end result for these rolls is a hybrid of a sticky bun and a cinnamon bun, with delightfully crunchy edges that give it a lovely Cinnamon Toast Crunch energy. If you feel moved to frost these rather than take my excellent advice about the maple syrup, skip the syrup and use the Salty Vanilla Frosting (page 293).

This recipe is sort of an outlier in this book (it takes so long, there's all that kneading and proofing and baking), but I know so many "nonbakers" who have had excellent success with it that I feel confident it's still perfectly at home among easy recipes like one-bowl cakes and "ice cream in melon." I believe in these cinnamon rolls and I believe in you!

sticky cinnamon rolls

Makes 12 rolls

For the dough

1 cup/240g whole milk or buttermilk

¼ cup/55g granulated sugar

1 (7g) envelope active dry yeast (2¼ teaspoons)

3¾ cups/545g all-purpose flour

1½ teaspoons/6g baking powder

1½ teaspoons/6g kosher salt

2 large eggs

1 stick/4 ounces/115g unsalted butter, cold or at room temperature, cut into ½-inch pieces

Cooking spray, softened butter, or neutral oil, for the bowl

For the filling and assembly

Cooking spray or softened butter, for the pan

⅔ cup/200g maple syrup, plus more for brushing

1 cup/220g light brown sugar

1 tablespoon ground cinnamon

¾ teaspoon/3g kosher salt

All-purpose flour, for dusting

1 stick/4 ounces/115g unsalted butter, at room temperature or melted and cooled

Flaky sea salt (optional)

1 **Make the dough:** In the bowl of a stand mixer, use a handheld whisk to blend the milk, sugar, and yeast together.

2 Throw the dough hook attachment onto the mixer, and add the flour, baking powder, and salt. Mix on low until the dough starts to come together in a dry, shaggy mess. Add the eggs, one at a time, and mix on medium speed until you've got a smooth, sticky dough with no visible dry spots (occasionally stop the machine, scraping the bottom of the bowl with a spatula or dough scraper to make sure all the dry bits of flour are incorporated).

3 With the mixer running, add the butter a few pieces at a time, letting it incorporate before adding more. Eventually, the dough will take all the butter, disappearing into a silky, sticky mass. Knead on medium for 3–4 minutes until it's slightly less sticky, appearing smooth and bulbous, like a new bowling ball. It'll start making a delightful slapping sound as it's fully kneaded—listen for it.

4 Grease a medium bowl with cooking spray and place the dough inside, immediately covering with plastic. Refrigerate for 12–24 hours. During this time, the dough is slowly rising (developing excellent flavor), the flour is hydrating, and the butter is resolidifying, making the dough easy to roll out.

5 **Make the filling and get ready to assemble:** Once you're ready to bake, prepare the filling and your workspace for THE ASSEMBLY (i.e., make sure you have a clean countertop, free of clutter).

6 Grease a 3-quart/9 ×13-inch baking dish with cooking spray, pour in the maple syrup, and swirl to coat the bottom. (Or use two 9-inch cake pans or one 9-inch cake pan and one 8 × 4-inch loaf pan.)

7 In a medium bowl, combine the brown sugar, cinnamon, and kosher salt.

8 Remove the dough from the fridge. It should be firm, and not at all sticky. (See? Magic!)

9 Lightly flour your work surface and, using a rolling pin or wine bottle or whatever, roll the dough into a rectangle about 12 × 24 inches, lifting the dough and lightly flouring underneath as needed to prevent sticking.

A cup of strong coffee, a plate of nice fruit, some salty sausage. Très continental!

Do ahead

The dough can be made 2 days ahead before assembling and baking. Or, if you prefer, the buns can be assembled in their pan, refrigerated, and then proofed/baked the next day.

10 Using an offset spatula or back of a spoon, spread the softened butter onto the full surface of the dough (or brush on with a pastry brush if butter is melted). Scatter the brown sugar mixture on top, and, like you're playing in sand, run your hand over it to lightly pack and evenly distribute.

11 Set the rectangle with a long side facing you. Start at the edge nearest to you and roll the dough up, pressing and tucking lightly. Work quickly here, as the dough will have been out of the fridge for a while, making it trickier to work with. Don't rush, but . . . you know.

12 Cut the dough in half so you have two logs roughly 12 inches each. Cut each log of dough into six 2-inch-wide pieces. Don't worry if the slices are imperfect—they'll plump up and resolve themselves as they proof and bake.

13 Place the cinnamon rolls in your chosen baking dish, swirl sides facing up. They'll be pretty spaced apart and may appear sparse or lonely—they'll get closer as they proof, even closer when they bake.

14 Cover the pans with plastic wrap. (If you're planning on baking these later, or if you're only baking one of two pans, store the rolls in the fridge.) Place the wrapped pan(s) of cinnamon rolls in a gently warm place (on top of the oven, fridge, or radiator are popular) and let the rolls proof until they're puffed and almost doubled in size, 35–40 minutes—they should definitely all be touching now. (If your rolls are coming directly from the fridge, this may take closer to 60 minutes.)

15 Meanwhile, position a rack in the center of the oven and preheat the oven to 350°F.

16 Remove the plastic wrap and bake the rolls until they are puffed and deeply golden brown on the edges and into the centers, 35–40 minutes for the 9 × 13 baking dish, closer to 30–35 minutes for two pans. They should feel firm on the edges, but still a little squishy toward the center.

17 Once out of the oven, immediately brush the rolls with a bit more maple syrup, just to "glaze" them. This must happen when they are hot; otherwise, the syrup will stay "wet" instead of "sticky." Sprinkle with flaky salt and let cool slightly before eating.

sweet enough scones

½ cup/120g heavy cream,
plus more for brushing

½ cup/110g sour cream

2 cups/290g all-purpose flour,
plus more for the work surface

⅓ cup/70g sugar,
plus more for sprinkling

1 tablespoon/12g baking powder

1¼ teaspoons/5g kosher salt

1 stick/4 ounces/115g cold
unsalted butter, cut into small
pieces

2½ cups/300g raspberries
or blueberries, chopped
strawberries, or halved
blackberries

Flaky sea salt, to finish

Eat with
A cup of something caffeinated,
with honey butter, or bring on a
hike or outdoors for a cute brunch.

Do ahead
The dough can be made
6-8 hours ahead, then covered
and refrigerate. Scones can be
baked a few hours ahead. Reheat
before serving, if desired.

I will hand it to them—scones always look great. But after being burned at every turn, one triangle of compacted sand after another, I couldn't help but wonder: Are scones bad? A sobering truth, but yes. Scones are bad. Scones are dry. Scones disappoint. Sure, I've had EXCELLENT scones (hi, Tandem Bakery in Portland, Maine!), but they are far and few between. But I always order them, because I so badly believe in the concept. A slightly more firm muffin? A sweeter, fruity biscuit? Sign me up for all of the above.

So, I present: *these* scones. These scones are different, with so much fat that the flour is really just there as a courtesy, and more fruit than you suspect will fit, but it does, lending flavor *and* moisture. They are puffy, fluffy, and downright cloud-like. Tender without being cakey, and gorgeously deformed (on purpose), because anything that holds a perfect triangle shape is not to be trusted. They're great, and I hope they change your mind about scones. I know they changed mine.

1   Preheat the oven to 425°F. Line a baking sheet with parchment paper.

2   In a small bowl, mix together the heavy cream and sour cream. In a large bowl, whisk together the flour, sugar, baking powder, and kosher salt.

3   Using your hands, add the butter and smash it into the flour to get large-ish, flat, even pieces (most of the butter should be smushed, resembling flakes, rather than large chunks), not unlike pie dough before you add water, or biscuits before the buttermilk. Add the raspberries and toss to coat. Using a spoon, stir in the sour cream mixture and then use your hands to gently knead a few times just until a shaggy dough comes together (the berries will get crushed here, that's okay).

4   Lightly flour your countertop and pat the dough into a rectangle about 6 × 9 inches, 2-1½ inches thick. Cut it in half lengthwise, then in half crosswise to make 4 pieces. Cut each piece in half on the diagonal so you've got 8 triangles. Place the scones on the lined baking sheet about 1 inch apart. For extra fluffy scones, refrigerate 20–30 minutes before baking.

5   Brush a little cream on top of the scones and sprinkle with sugar. Bake until golden brown on the tops and bottoms, 25–30 minutes.

cheesy, salty, savory scones

Makes 8 scones

½ cup/120g heavy cream, plus more for brushing

½ cup/110g sour cream

1¾ cups/255g all-purpose flour, plus more for the work surface

1½ cups/125g finely grated parmesan or pecorino cheese, plus more for sprinkling

2-3 teaspoons coarsely ground black pepper, plus more for sprinkling

1 tablespoon/12g baking powder

1 tablespoon/12g sugar

1¼ teaspoons/5g kosher salt

1 medium leek or 6 scallions, white and light-green parts only, very thinly sliced

¼ cup/12g finely chopped fresh dill (optional)

1 stick/4 ounces/115g cold unsalted butter, cut into small pieces

Flaky sea salt

Eat with
Fried eggs, sausage (links, not patties), an entire stick of softened butter.

Do ahead
The dough can be made 6-8 hours ahead, then covered and refrigerated. The scones can be baked a few hours ahead. Reheat before serving, if desired.

This feels like a weird thing to casually drop in the middle of a dessert book, but: I absolutely, 100 percent, will always and forever prefer savory to sweet. I would rather eat an onion than an apple, lick salt than sugar. In case you feel the same, first, thank you for buying this book anyway, I hope it inspires you to give some sweet things a try. Second, you will adore this recipe. I believe in a heavy cream/sour cream-based scone rather than a laminated scone (which to me, is more of a biscuit); what you lose in "flakiness," you make up for in richness, tenderness, and never-dryness.

1   Preheat the oven to 425°F. Line a baking sheet with parchment paper.

2   In a small bowl, mix together the heavy cream and sour cream. In a large bowl, whisk together the flour, parmesan, pepper, baking powder, sugar, kosher salt, all but a small handful of leeks (you can use these reserved pieces to top the scones before baking), and dill (if using) until well blended.

3   Using your hands (never a food processor!), add the butter and smash the butter into the flour to get large-ish, flat, even pieces—most of the butter should be smushed, resembling flakes, rather than large chunks or cubes, not unlike pie dough before you add water, or biscuits before the buttermilk.

4   Using a spoon, stir in the sour cream mixture and then use your hands to gently knead a few times just until a shaggy dough comes together.

5   Lightly flour the countertop and turn the dough onto it, patting it into a rectangle about 6 × 9 inches and about 1½ inches thick. Cut it in half lengthwise, then in half crosswise to make 4 pieces. Cut each piece in half on the diagonal so you've got 8 triangles. Place the scones on the prepared baking sheet about 1 inch apart. For extra fluffy scones (or if the dough is feeling particularly soft/it's particularly warm in your kitchen), refrigerate 20–30 minutes before baking.

6   Brush a little cream on top of the scones, sprinkle with sea salt and more pepper, and scatter a few reserved rings of the light-green part of the leek on top. Bake until golden brown on the tops and bottoms, 25–30 minutes.

cornbread

Makes one 9-inch cornbread

1 stick/4 ounces/115g unsalted butter, melted, plus more softened butter for serving

1 cup/145g all-purpose flour

1 cup/130g coarse cornmeal

½ cup/90g packed light brown sugar

1 tablespoon/12g baking powder

1¼ teaspoons/5g kosher salt

1 teaspoon coarsely ground black pepper (optional)

2 large eggs

¾ cup/170g mayonnaise, sour cream, or a mix of both

½ cup/120g buttermilk

Honey, for serving

Flaky sea salt, for serving

Eat with
A four-bean salad, a bowl of pozole or chili, a summer tomato salad, a giant beer on ice.

Do ahead
The cornbread can be baked 2 days ahead, tightly wrapped in plastic, and stored at room temperature. It'll last up to 5 days in the fridge, but you'll want to toast in butter or griddle it before serving.

Note
The mayo keeps the cornbread moist, enhances the color, and gives it a unique crust that almost seems fried.

You may have some "thoughts" about this cornbread. First, if you are the sort who believes cornbread should be strictly savory, nary a whisper of sugar, baked in nothing but a pool of bacon grease inside a cast-iron skillet, flip the page. This is not going to make you happy. If you believe cornbread, like any other quick-bread-type delicacy, should have just enough sugar to balance out the salt, baked in whatever the hell you have on hand, then I think you're going to absolutely love it.

Second, there is mayonnaise in this cornbread. Please do not let this freak you out—mayonnaise is just oil and eggs (two ingredients typically found in cornbread), so it really isn't that strange if you think about it. Are you still thinking about it? If you simply can't fathom the addition, sour cream also works. But please, try to trust me on this one.

1   Preheat the oven to 400°F.

2   Spoon a bit (a tablespoon or so) of the melted butter into the bottom of a 9-inch pie plate, cake pan, or cast-iron skillet (any 1-quart/1-liter baking dish). Using a brush or your fingers (I am using my fingers), grease the dish all along the bottom and up the sides.

3   In a medium bowl, whisk together the flour, cornmeal, brown sugar, baking powder, salt, and pepper (if using).

4   In another medium bowl or measuring cup, whisk together the eggs, mayonnaise, and buttermilk.

5   Whisk the wet ingredients into the dry ingredients, but just until combined (a few dry spots/lumps are okay). Add the remaining melted butter to the batter and gently fold until it's totally incorporated.

6   Pour the batter into the prepared pan, smooth the top, and bake until the edges are deeply browned and crispy and the top is a lovely, sunflower-y golden yellow color (if it cracks, I'm into that), 20–25 minutes.

7   Remove from oven and let cool a few minutes before slicing into. While you wait, if you like, mix some softened butter with a good amount of honey and a healthy pinch of flaky salt. Mix until shiny, glossy, and spreadable and serve with the cornbread.

perfect pancakes, perfect waffles

Serves 4-6

2 cups/290g all-purpose flour

3 tablespoons/40g sugar

1½ teaspoons/6g baking powder

1½ teaspoons/9g baking soda

1¼ teaspoons/5g kosher salt

2⅓ cups/550g buttermilk

2 large eggs

4 tablespoons/2 ounces/55g
unsalted butter, melted,
plus more for serving

1 cup/150g blueberries or
2 bananas, sliced (optional)

Coconut oil, ghee, canola oil,
or vegetable oil, for cooking
the pancakes

Eat with
Maple syrup and a bowl of fresh
fruit, for health.

Do ahead
The batter can be made 2 hours
ahead and kept refrigerated.
While nothing beats a fresh
pancake, you can actually freeze
cooked pancakes, reviving them
later by popping them into a
toaster oven.

Every time I revisit this one, try to tweak it, or make an improvement, I conclude that it's still the best pancake recipe I know. Brown and crispy on the outsides, soft, borderline custardy on the insides, they're just sweet enough, still begging for a generous dip into a pool of maple syrup.

These pancakes have been previously described as "pancakes for waffle people," but they could also just be described as "waffles," since the batter works gorgeously in a waffle iron (Belgian, square, deep pockets, shallow pockets, etc). Waffles are admittedly easier (step 1: put batter in the waffle iron) while pancakes require a bit of finesse, adjustment, and trial and error.

So, if you're making pancakes, the first key for pancake success is to make sure you've got plenty of fat inside a hot skillet. You should hear the batter sizzling immediately upon dropping—you're effectively frying the batter as it rises and puffs, flipping only once it's got a sturdy base, so it doesn't deflate. The second key is to give yourself the grace and allowance to make one (or two) test pancakes while you figure out the right heat and amount of batter. These first pancakes will not be gorgeous and they will not be right. They might be burned or undercooked, or sometimes both. These first pancakes are the testers, and the sooner you accept this as part of the pancake-making process, the better time you'll have.

To serve, I encourage you to think of a pancake or waffle as another version of a biscuit or something. Are all three perfect simply with a smear of butter, a dousing of maple syrup, and a sprinkle of flaky salt? Absolutely. Could both go in any number of directions, sweet and savory? I think they can, and I think you should.

Waffles with a good spread of cream cheese, labne, or full-fat Greek yogurt, salt and pepper, thinly sliced scallions, and smoked fish on the side would please me. I have enjoyed pancakes with ricotta, dipped in very thick honey. Full English waffle breakfast (with crisp bacon, fat sausages, jammy egg, roasted tomatoes) is not something I've ever had but think sounds good.

1   In a large bowl, whisk together the flour, sugar, baking powder, baking soda, and salt.

2   In a medium bowl (or the measuring cup you measured your buttermilk in), whisk the buttermilk and eggs together. Gently whisk this mixture into your dry ingredients—it's okay if more than a few lumps remain. Add the melted butter and (still) gently whisk everything together, moving toward the outside of the bowl, until all ingredients are incorporated. Do not overbeat (a few lumps are fine, trust!). Mix in the fruit, if using. (If you like, the batter at this stage can be refrigerated for an hour or two.)

3   **For pancakes,** heat a large nonstick griddle or skillet (preferably cast-iron if not nonstick) over medium heat for a few minutes, until the skillet is very hot. Add 1–2 tablespoons oil to the skillet and reduce the heat to medium-low. Using a measuring cup, ladle ¼–⅓ cup/60ml–80ml batter into the skillet (depending on how large you like your pancakes). If you're using a large skillet (or a griddle), feel free to make one or two more at a time, making sure they aren't spreading together to make one giant pancake. Once you notice a few bubbles begin rising on the surface of the pancakes and the bottoms are nicely browned (this will take 2–4 minutes), flip them. Cook until the other sides are lightly browned, another 2 minutes or so.

3   **For waffles,** follow the instructions per your specific waffle maker and make those waffles!

4   If you're making a bunch at a time, you can move the pancakes or waffles as they're ready to a wire rack set inside a sheet pan, and keep them in a 300°F oven until all the batter is cooked and you're ready to serve (I also don't think pancakes or waffles need to always be served warm, so no need to do this step if you agree).

Xuans Crepes

		1/2
400 g	A.P.	200g
120 g	sugar	60g
5 g	salt	pinch
8	eggs	4
4	yolks	2
1 L	milk	1/2
150 g	brown butter	75g

thin maple pancakes

Serves 4-6

6 tablespoons/3 ounces/85g
unsalted butter,
plus more for serving

1½ cups/220g all-purpose flour

2 tablespoons/25g sugar

1 teaspoon/4g kosher salt

1¼ cups/29g whole milk

4 large eggs

⅓ cup/100g maple syrup,
plus more for serving

Neutral oil, for cooking the
pancakes

Lemon wedges, for serving

Eat with
Sliced fresh citrus or very crispy
bacon after a fun sleepover.

Do ahead
The batter can be made 1 day
ahead and stored airtight in the
refrigerator.

Note
Make the first pancake to
calibrate your preferences and
work out the kinks. If the first
pancake does not come out
perfectly, do not despair. If it's
too brown, turn the heat down
or flip it sooner. If it's too light,
turn the heat up or flip it later. If it
sticks, use more oil or let the pan
get hotter. If it's too thick, add a
little milk to the batter. If it's too
thin (though I don't think this will
be), whisk in a little more flour.
Let the first pancake inform your
journey, and always feel free to
adjust from there.

Xuan ran the sister bakery of the first restaurant I worked at, and his brown butter crepes were both the first and best thing I learned to make. They were fussy, requiring a hand blender, a fine-mesh sieve, an overnight rest in the fridge, and a carbon-steel crepe pan. They took weeks for me to get right—the swirl in the pan, correct heat, proper browning.

At the restaurant, we'd heat butter in a skillet and lightly fry the crepe, then hit it with a small ladle of simple syrup, which glazed and caramelized the edges in their brown butter bath. It became so crispy, it held its shape like a crumpled napkin. We served it with warmed fruits glazed in their own juices and a scoop of ice cream.

Anyway, sorry to get you excited, but these are not those. But these are inspired by and close enough. Less fussy, slightly thicker, but with the same fun lacy edges (thanks to the addition of maple syrup) and so, so much brown butter.

1   In a small pot or skillet, melt the butter over medium heat. Let it come to a sizzle and whisk occasionally, scraping up any browned bits forming on the bottom of the pot or skillet. Remove from the heat.

2   In a large bowl, whisk together the flour, sugar, and salt.

3   In a medium bowl, whisk together the milk, eggs, and syrup. Slowly pour the milk mixture into the flour mixture and gently whisk just until no lumps remain. Add the browned butter and whisk to blend.

4   In a medium skillet (nonstick, regular, or cast-iron all work here), heat a touch of neutral oil over medium-high heat. Add about ¼ cup/60ml of batter to the skillet and let it spread as it wants to in a wild, flower-esque pattern (the batter will be slightly thicker than crepe batter, so don't expect the pancake to be quite as thin). Cook until browned and frizzled at the ends, 1½–2 minutes.

5   Flip the pancake to cook on the other side, 30–60 seconds. Try it—if you wish it was a little thinner, add a splash of milk to the batter and try again.

6   Serve with more butter, maple syrup, and a squeeze of lemon.

fun lacy edges

toasted oat and honey cobbler

Serves 6–8

Anytime shortcake dough for breakfast cobbler, page 95

For the filling

2 pounds/910g apricots, plums, peaches, or nectarines, halved (or quartered if very large)

¼–⅓ cup/90g–120g honey*

2 tablespoons cornstarch

2–3 tablespoons fresh lime or lemon juice*

Pinch of kosher salt

For assembly

Heavy cream, for brushing

Flaky sea salt, for sprinkling

Rolled oats or quick-cooking oats, for sprinkling

Sugar, for sprinkling

*Add more or less honey and citrus juice depending on the needs of the fruit.

Eat with
Whipped cream or 50/50 (Tangy Whipped Cream, page 279)! Pistachio or vanilla ice cream!

Do ahead
This cobbler is truly best the day it's made, but it can be stored tightly wrapped at room temperature and eaten throughout the next few days if you like.

It cannot be denied that the absolute best time to serve a cobbler is after an outdoor summer dinner—where you've mostly eaten things like tomatoes and anchovies—brought out just before it gets dark, to be enjoyed with a few bottles of juicy wine. So, why is this cobbler in the breakfast chapter? Because aside from that, I truly consider cobbler to be a breakfast food. That's it. It's après *midsommar* dinner or it's breakfast. If you dissect the components you're looking at a biscuit-y topping (biscuits are breakfast) and jammy fruit (jam, also a breakfast food). 1 + 1 = 2, I don't make the rules!

As for this particular cobbler, I want you to read the recipe and then feel empowered to ignore it completely. If you think of a cobbler as less of a recipe and more of a concept, you'll open yourself up to a wild world of possibilities. I am partial to the oat-y topping for a breakfast cobbler (toast the oats, or don't, but if you do, you'll be glad you did!), or you can go the classic shortcake or cornmeal varieties (use the anytime shortcake recipes on page 94–95).

1   Preheat the oven to 350°F.

2   Prepare breakfast cobbler variation of the Anytime Shortcake Dough (page 94).

3   **Prepare the filling:** In a 2-quart (2-liter) baking dish (an 8 × 11-inch or 9 × 13-inch dish will work), toss the fruit with the honey, cornstarch, lime juice, and kosher salt, then flip the fruit so they are all cut-side up. The fruit may overlap a bit, and this is fine.

4   **To assemble:** Top the fruit with the shortcakes, which will puff and spread quite a bit, so leave them well spaced (the idea is to have lots of fruit exposed once baked). Brush the shortcakes with cream and sprinkle with flaky sea salt and a bit more oats and sugar.

5   Bake until the shortcakes are golden brown and the juices of the fruit have thickened and bubbled up around the edges of the baking dish, 45–50 minutes.

6   Let cool slightly before eating (though it's even better at room temperature).

a better banana bread

Makes one 9 × 4-inch loaf

Cooking spray or softened butter and granulated sugar, for the pan (optional)

1½ cups/218g all-purpose flour

1 teaspoon baking soda

¾ teaspoon/3g kosher salt

1 stick/4 ounces/113g butter, at room temperature

½ cup/110g granulated sugar, plus 2–3 tablespoons

½ cup/110g light brown sugar

2 large eggs

3 very ripe bananas/320g, peeled and mashed, plus 1 banana, halved lengthwise

½ cup/100g mascarpone, whole-milk yogurt, or sour cream

Eat with
Sliced and toasted, smeared with softened butter, and sprinkled with salt. Also good used as the base of a banana split with A Very Good Chocolate Sauce (page 284) or Crunchy Chocolate Sauce (page 285).

Do ahead
The banana bread can be baked 1 week ahead, tightly wrapped, and stored in the refrigerator (or wrapped tightly in foil and frozen for up to 1 month).

I've been carrying around this recipe for twenty years. It's modified from Michel Bras's *Notebooks*, a book I pored over as a young cook. Nearly all the recipes were unmakeable ("makeability" wasn't really his point), but one looked doable: a banana bread. So I made it, made it again, tweaked it to suit a regular kitchen with regular ingredients, and here we are. Banana bread is a staple, something you should have a reliable recipe for. Some don't require a mixer; this one does. I promise it's worth it for the delicate cakey texture and crispy, almost honeycomb-like exterior. It freezes beautifully and keeps on the counter for a full week, deepening in flavor as it sits—three-day-old banana bread is better than day-of, and you can quote me on that.

1   Preheat the oven to 350°F. Line a 9 × 4-inch loaf pan with parchment paper. (Alternatively, spray a 9 × 4-inch loaf pan with cooking spray or grease with softened butter and sprinkle the interior with enough granulated sugar to coat, tapping out excess—this will give you a slightly sweeter banana bread with a crunchy crust.)

2   In a medium bowl, whisk together the flour, baking soda, and salt.

3   In a stand mixer fitted with the paddle (or in a medium bowl with an electric hand mixer), cream the butter, ½ cup/110g sugar, and the light brown sugar together until light and fluffy, 3–5 minutes. Add the eggs, one at a time. Beat until light and fluffy, another 3–5 minutes. Slowly add the flour mixture, scraping down the sides of the bowl until everything is mostly incorporated (do not overmix).

4   Add the mashed bananas and mascarpone and mix until well blended, making sure to get all the batter at the bottom of the bowl. Transfer the batter to the prepared loaf pan, top with the halved banana, cut-side up, and sprinkle with the remaining 2–3 tablespoons sugar.

5   Bake until the bread is puffed up, golden brown, and starting to pull away from the sides of the pan, 1 hour 10 minutes to 1 hour 20 minutes. (Yes, this bakes for a long time—loaf cakes, especially very moist ones, take awhile. Do not rush it or it will almost certainly collapse on you!) Let cool completely before slicing or wrapping for later.

I give away 90 percent of the desserts I make, which I chalk up to several personality traits, a robust social life, and perhaps, most obviously, my profession. Not like, for a raffle or anything—more like for a housewarming, congratulations on a new baby, happy birthday, sorry you broke up, or, more often, simply because I happen to be recipe testing and would they like a buttermilk pie with a small slice already removed and two quarts of salted chocolate pudding?

Desserts were made to be gifted, made to travel. They're certainly easier to move around than, say, a roasted chicken or a shrimp cocktail (I've gifted/transported both). I've put desserts on subways, in the backseats of taxis, on a ferry (!), and in the passenger seat of my own car (yes, they always wear a seatbelt). Despite how tenderly they are tucked in or preciously cradled, there is always the sinking feeling that I will Ruin The Dessert. That it'll spill in the bag when the car takes a hard right, get crushed by something (I don't know what), or dropped onto the subway platform like at least one pair of sunglasses and two single AirPods. Mid-trip, I'll wonder, "Should I really have brought this dessert on [insert transit mode here]? A bottle of wine would have been a fine thing to bring. Why did I have to bring [insert dessert here]?" I am very clumsy and it feels like Mercury is always in retrograde.

Of course, disasters do happen. I've walked through the doors of my nearest and dearest with an exploding container of pastry cream, and once I sheepishly gifted a container of crushed cookies to a mother-to-be. Luckily, my friendships have not suffered as a consequence, and the desserts, perfectly imperfect or perhaps just imperfect, are always welcomed with open arms. "It's the thought that counts," but if the frosting got smudged or even if the pie crust got smudged, it's also the work and effort that counts. When something is made with love and care, it can only ever be half-ruined.

So yes, the answer to "Should I really try to bring this dessert with me?" should always be "Of course." And when you do: Use foil to wrap it more times than you think—it's practically thin sheet metal and stronger than it ought to be. Whip the cream on location or bring separately; otherwise, topping and transporting a pie will not end well. If the galette/pie/cake/cobbler is too hot to hold, don't bring it, sorry. Trifles are an especially good thing to bring—all components packed separately like some sort of fantasy picnic to be assembled upon arrival. Cookies can be packed in a long plastic container lined with paper towels to avoid rattling around. Wrap cakes in parchment like wrapping paper— a note or little flower tucked into some butcher's twine is a nice touch and will say, "This gift is intentional," and not, "Please take this banana bread off my hands. I can't eat any more banana bread this week."

have dessert will travel

staples and extras

Think of these recipes as your building blocks, the staples, the basics. While these things aren't necessarily used multiple times in the book, they are invaluable to anyone's dessert repertoire. Crusts to be made sweet or savory; a crumble topping to be baked on top of pies, turned into a crisp, or eaten on its own over roasted fruit; sauces you can put on ice cream, pies, or just a spoon. You'll be glad to have these undeniably simple and gratifying recipes in your back pocket to sass up any number of things you may have bought or made.

Someone once told me I only like to do things if they are hard, and while there is some truth to that, I should say that I only like to do hard things if that's the best way to do them. Many things that are harder than another way also happen to be better than another way. So be it!

Whipping cream by hand is one of those things. When I was twenty-three, my new boss, William, saw me splashing heavy cream into the bowl of a stand mixer and letting it rip on speed four. He turned the machine off and made me promise never to whip cream in a stand mixer ever again. You have never seen anyone so horrified as this man than when he saw his new, probably hungover, employee whipping cream in a stand mixer. Since I was the type of insufferable learner who could only accept instruction if I knew the HOW and WHY behind it, I required a full-blown lesson in the mechanics of fat and water separation, why faster was not better, why the heat from the machine could affect the end result, and why it was frankly embarrassing and unprofessional to not whip your cream by hand (I still can't find the data to back up the last claim).

But I am not here to shame, only to offer an alternative if you have never whipped cream by hand. The side-by-side comparison will reveal a difference that is noticeable and drastic, if you ask me. In a stand mixer, there is ease, but there is also force, which gives you more of a grainy "this will turn into cheese if I keep going" texture. By hand it takes a different kind of force (from your arms), and sure, it takes longer, but there is also a gentleness to the whipped cream, a suppleness, a something that says cloud-like, it says pillowy, it says dreamy.

Aside from an end result being what I would describe as "higher quality," there's a meditative element to whipping cream by hand. Like many things in my life, it's also about the quest for control and intimacy. I find that getting closer to the ingredients keeps you more in touch with the end product. (I'd rather lie down in the street than let anything that plugs in touch my pie dough.)

Whipping the cream in a stainless steel bowl (a wider bowl will make it happen faster) with a whisk (I like the classic shape, not tapered and not balloon), you feel it change, feel it going from liquid to solid, from heavy to ethereal with each back and forth of the whisk. You can take a break, if you like (the arms do get tired), and you may think it will never change (it will), but all of a sudden, you have whipped cream. First, the softest of soft peaks, barely perceptible but decidedly no longer pourable heavy cream. Then, you'll travel to medium peaks, but not quite stiff enough to sit proudly atop that tart you just baked, and then, truly like magic, you've got a bowl of perfectly whipped cream.

Try it for yourself and you, too, might become someone who likes to do things the hard way.

whipping cream by hand

50/50
(tangy whipped cream)

Makes about 2 cups/ enough for one 9-inch pie

1 cup/235ml heavy cream

1 cup/290g whole-milk Greek yogurt or full-fat sour cream

⅓ cup/40g powdered sugar

Small pinch of kosher salt

Eat with
Every dessert under the sun.

Do ahead
Best made right before using.

This is my default topping and accompaniment for most desserts that would otherwise use whipped cream. This is not to knock classic whipped cream (it is, as you know, perfect), but simply to offer an alternative when you wished there was a bit more . . . something going on. A bit more tanginess, acidity, depth. The yogurt (or sour cream, if it suits you) also adds a density that seems like it would be counterintuitive to the light airiness desired by whipped cream, but it really really does work. Oh, and it doubles well, if the need strikes.

1 In a medium bowl, using a whisk (or, if you really would like, an electric hand mixer), whisk the heavy cream until it's starting to thicken and has soft, medium peaks, 2–4 minutes or so.

2 Add the yogurt, powdered sugar, and salt and continue to whisk until it looks like gorgeous, pillowy whipped cream (you'll know when you know), another 2–3 minutes.

the only pie crust

Makes 2 discs

2½ cups/362g all-purpose flour,
plus more for rolling

2 teaspoons/8g sugar

1 teaspoon/4g kosher salt

2½ sticks/10 ounces/285g
unsalted butter, cut into 1-inch
pieces, chilled

1 tablespoon/15g apple cider
vinegar or distilled white vinegar

¼ cup/60g ice cold water, plus
more only if you absolutely must

Use for
Pies, galettes sweet and savory,
hand pies, Pop-Tarts.

Do ahead
The pie dough can be made and
refrigerated for up to 1 week;
frozen for up to 2 months.

I believe in this recipe so much that I keep republishing it every chance I get, in every book I write. It's flaky, it's buttery, it doesn't require a food processor (in fact, I'd recommend against using one) and 98 percent of people who have made it have success with it 100 percent of the time. My tip here is to resist the urge to add more water—pie dough should never look like a smooth, shiny dough. The flour in the dough will hydrate as it sits, transforming from shaggy to more supple once rested. Remember, pie crusts are meant to be flaky, shatteringly crisp. Not doughy or cookie-like. Keep that in mind when the dough looks, well . . . flaky. That's a good sign!

1 In a large bowl, whisk together the flour, sugar, and salt. Add the butter and toss to coat it in the flour mixture. Using your hands, smash the butter between your palms and fingertips, mixing it into the flour, creating long, thin, flaky, floury, buttery bits. Once most of the butter is incorporated and there are no large chunks remaining, dump the flour mixture onto a work surface.

2 In a measuring cup, combine the vinegar and ice water and drizzle it over the flour/butter mixture. Run your fingers through the mixture like you're running your fingers through your hair, just to evenly distribute the water through the flour until the dough starts coming together.

3 Knead the dough a few more times, just to gather up any dry bits from the bottom and place them on the top to be incorporated. You will be tempted to add a tablespoon or two more water now—resist if you can, add only if you must.

4 Once you've got a shaggy mass of dough (it will not be smooth and it certainly will not be shiny), knead it once or twice more and divide it in half. Pat each piece into a flat disc about 1 inch thick. Wrap each disc individually in plastic wrap and refrigerate at least 2 hours.

whole wheat pie crust

Makes 2 discs

1¾ cups/255g all-purpose flour

¾ cup/100g whole wheat, spelt, or rye flour

2 teaspoons/8g sugar

1½ teaspoons/6g kosher salt

2½ sticks/10 ounces/285g unsalted butter, cut into 1-inch pieces, chilled

1 tablespoon/15g apple cider vinegar or distilled white vinegar

⅓ cup/80g ice cold water, plus more only if you absolutely must

Use for
Sweet and savory galettes, quiche, pot pie, tomato tart.

Do ahead
The pie dough can be made and refrigerated for up to 1 week; frozen for up to 2 months.

While I still believe in the power of The Only Pie Crust (opposite), this is a great variation. I am not a whole-grain baking specialist, by any means, but I do like to occasionally dabble in swapping a percentage of all-purpose with whole wheat or alternative grain flours, such as rye or spelt flour. for added nuttiness, complexity, and a slightly grittier texture. While stone fruit and berry galettes do play well in this type of environment, my favorite application for whole wheat/whole grains is for savory galettes and quiches. Something to keep in mind is that whole-grain flours absorb moisture differently than refined white flour, so there is a bit more water in this recipe than the classic version to keep things properly hydrated. For this reason, you may find yourself adding a bit more flour when rolling out (you can use all-purpose for that), which is totally fine.

1 In a large bowl, whisk together the flours, sugar, and salt. Add the butter and toss to coat it in the flour mixture. Using your hands, smash the butter between your palms and fingertips, mixing it into the flour, creating long, thin, flaky, floury, buttery bits. Once most of the butter is incorporated and there are no large chunks remaining, dump the flour mixture onto a work surface.

2 In a measuring cup, combine the vinegar and ice water and drizzle it over the flour/butter mixture. Run your fingers through the mixture like you're running your fingers through your hair, just to evenly distribute the water through the flour until the dough starts coming together.

3 Knead the dough a few more times, just to gather up any dry bits from the bottom and place them on the top to be incorporated. You will be tempted to add a tablespoon or two more water now—resist if you can, add only if you must.

4 Once you've got a shaggy mass of dough (it will not be smooth and it certainly will not be shiny), knead it once or twice more and divide it in half. Pat each piece into a flat disc about 1 inch thick. Wrap each disc individually in plastic wrap and refrigerate at least 2 hours.

a very good chocolate sauce

Makes 1½ cups

½ cup/55g unsweetened cocoa powder, preferably dark

¼ cup/55g sugar

3 ounces/85g bittersweet chocolate (at least 68% cacao), chopped

Kosher salt

Eat with
Ice cream, ice cream cake, chocolate cake, chocolate ice cream cake.

Do ahead
It's dairy-free, so it will ostensibly keep in your refrigerator for a long time. Because I'm not the FDA, let's call it 3 months, but I'll bet it's fine for much longer than that.

While it may seem impossible that the best version of chocolate sauce only requires you to pour boiling water over a bowl of stuff, I'm pleased to report it's true. This chocolate sauce is not temperamental and you don't need knowledge about working with chocolate to make it, just a bowl and a whisk.

One thing I will warn you about: This sauce is the perfect texture when it's warm-ish-to-room temperature. (Plus, hot chocolate sauce on my ice cream makes my ice cream melt too soon, and I hate that.) But for those who intend to enjoy their chocolate sauce warm-to-hot, use ⅔ cup/160ml water instead of the full cup for a thicker viscosity.

1 In a medium pot, bring ⅔–1 cup/150g–235g water to a boil (use the smaller amount of water for a thicker sauce).

2 Meanwhile, in a heatproof medium bowl, combine the cocoa powder, sugar, chopped chocolate, and a good pinch of salt.

3 Once the water boils, pour it over the cocoa powder mixture and let sit a minute or two to start melting the chocolate. Whisk until smooth and shiny, season with more salt if you like that sort of thing.

4 That's it, that's the sauce.

crunchy chocolate sauce

Makes about 1½ cups

8 ounces/225g bittersweet chocolate (65%–72% cacao), chopped (about 1 cup)

1 cup/225g coconut oil

Kosher salt

Eat with
Ice cream, ice cream cake, chocolate cake, chocolate ice cream cake.

Do ahead
It's dairy-free, so will ostensibly keep in your refrigerator for a long time. Because I'm not the FDA, let's call it 3 months, but I'll bet it's fine for much longer than that. Rewarm in the microwave or a pot over low heat before using.

This is an at-home version of Magic Shell™ (a chocolate sauce that is liquid and pourable when warm and seizes to a paper-thin shell when in contact with something cold or frozen, like ice cream), recipes of which have been published in many places. I want to tell you there's something about this one that makes it different or special, but really, there's not, because in order to properly work, you can really only futz with the proportions so much, and turns out, 50/50 chocolate to coconut oil really is the best proportion for pourability and crunchiness.

1   In a heatproof medium bowl, combine the chocolate and coconut oil and place over a small pot of barely simmering water.

2   Melt, stirring occasionally, until no lumps remain and you've got an impossibly shiny, chocolaty sauce. (Alternatively, microwave in 30-second increments until the sauce is shiny and no lumps remain.) Season with salt and set aside.

3   To serve, pour over scoops of ice cream to suit your wants, needs, desires.

caramel for all occasions

1 cup/220g sugar

2 tablespoons/1 ounce/30g cold unsalted butter, cut into ½-inch pieces

¾ cup/175ml heavy cream

1 tablespoon flaky sea salt

Eat with
Ice cream, pudding, warm ginger cake (page 142).

Do ahead
Caramel can be made 2 weeks in advance and kept refrigerated. It will solidify once chilled, so rewarm it in a microwave or small pot to liquefy.

There was a time where caramel was so popular it nearly became synonymous with desserts, topping the list alongside "chocolate" as the number one flavor profile for sweet snacks. Caramel on ice cream. Salted caramel ice cream. Caramel on cakes. Cakes made with caramel. And I get it, the flavor is undeniable. Caramelizing sugar takes a useful yet one-dimensional ingredient (sugar) and adds complexity in the form of bitterness and liquidity (dry sugar is solid, caramelized is a liquid—that is cool!). It's bitter, it's adult, it's saucy, and it tastes good on nearly everything in this book. It isn't, however, especially home-cook friendly, especially if you've never done it before.

UNTIL NOW. Just kidding, it can still be tricky, but maybe this technique, known as "dry caramel," will help those who have faced issues in the past. As the name implies, this means that you're going to caramelize the sugar without the presence of water, which means no chance for the sugar to crystallize. This is how I was taught in professional kitchens, and only when I started reading magazines and books for home cooks did I come across the technique using water and cream of tartar or lemon juice or whatever, which STILL can present issues like crystallization even to the most careful of recipe followers.

So: A Caramel for All Occasions. Easy enough to make and have in your fridge to drizzle or top or sauce or whatever you want to do with it.

1   Heat half the sugar in a heavy, medium pot over medium. Once the sugar starts to melt and liquefy, gently stir the sugar using a wooden spoon or heatproof spatula until it's a nice golden-brown color, 2–4 minutes. (You want this to happen slowly to prevent the risk of burning.)

2   Scatter the remaining sugar on top and cook until all the sugar is totally liquefied and a dark amber color, like good maple syrup, 2–3 minutes.

3   Slowly whisk in the butter, letting it melt and bubble up around the caramel, which will also stop the cooking. In a slow, gentle stream, whisk in the heavy cream, taking care not to add it all at once or the sugar will seize, giving you hard-to-dissolve clumps. Bring the whole thing to a simmer to emulsify the caramel, add the salt, and remove from the heat.

tahini caramel

Makes about 2½ cups

1 cup/220g sugar

⅔ cup/160g tahini

Kosher salt or flaky sea salt

Eat with
Ice cream party, Sugar Plum Galette with Halva (page 44), Semolina Cake with Lemon and Fennel (page 115).

Do ahead
It's dairy-free, so will ostensibly keep in your refrigerator for a long time. Because I'm not the FDA, let's call it 3 months, but I'll bet it's fine for much longer than that.

I love this caramel so much for anyone, but especially those abstaining from dairy but who don't want to miss out on a creamy, silky, salty caramel sauce. The tahini takes the place of both the butter and the heavy cream, although you'd never guess either was missing. For those who are tahini averse, know that it's not overpowering. Caramelized sugar already has strong nutty, borderline bitter notes; the tahini only adds to the chorus while adding fat, which translates to creaminess.

1 In a heavy, medium pot, heat ½ cup/110g of the sugar over medium heat. Once the sugar starts to melt and liquefy, gently stir the sugar using a wooden spoon or heatproof spatula until it's a nice golden-brown color, 2–4 minutes. (You want this to happen slowly to prevent the risk of burning.)

2 Scatter the remaining ½ cup/110g sugar on top and cook until all the sugar is totally liquefied and a dark amber color, like good maple syrup, 2–3 minutes.

3 Slowly stir in ⅔ cup/160ml water, taking care not to add it all at once or the sugar will seize. Then add the tahini, mixing to blend well. Bring the whole thing to a simmer to emulsify the tahini into the sauce, season with salt, and remove from the heat.

salted nutty crumble

*Makes 1½ cups/enough for one
9-inch pie*

1½ cups/200g unsalted roasted nuts (almonds, walnuts, pecans, hazelnuts, or pistachios) or 1¼ cups rolled oats

⅔ cup/95g all-purpose flour

⅔ cup/140g light brown sugar

1½ teaspoons/6g kosher salt

1 stick/4 ounces/115g cold unsalted butter, cut into ½-inch pieces

Use for
Pies, crisps, crumbles, snacking, ice cream sundaes.

Do ahead
The crumble can be made and stored unbaked in a resealable container for up to 1 month in the freezer. Baked, it will last 1 week, stored airtight at room temperature.

This is as close to a crumble recipe as you'll get in this book because, well, they just aren't my preference as a genre of dessert. Crumble topping on pie, though: Yes. Crumble topping baked like granola and used to sprinkle on top of ice cream, yogurt, or eat out of hand when you need something sweet but don't feel like making the commitment to "full dessert": Absolutely yes. For me, nuts are always the crunchiest, most flavorful thing you can use to make a crumble topping, but oats are an option here, too. That said, yes, of course this topping works as a fruit crumble if that's your thing.

When possible, opt for unsalted roasted nuts. If you can't find them already roasted, give regular unsalted nuts a little pretoast for 8–10 minutes in a 350°F oven; it'll make all the difference in the world to your final product.

1   In a food processor, combine the nuts (or oats), flour, brown sugar, and salt and process until you've got a coarse crumb; you should still see pieces of nut. (Alternatively, finely chop the nuts by hand and mix in a bowl with the flour, brown sugar, and salt.)

2   Add the butter to the processor and pulse until it's evenly distributed and you've got a wet crumb. (Alternatively, rub the butter into the nut mixture with your hands until it's evenly distributed and you've got a wet crumb texture.)

To use as the top of a pie or crumble
Sprinkle directly onto the fruit and bake as instructed in Sour Cherry Crumble Pie (page 55) or use in lieu of the oat shortcakes to turn the cobbler into a crisp (page 271).

To use as a snack, sundae topping, or with roasted fruit and cream
Spread onto a sheet pan and bake at 375°F, tossing occasionally, until the mixture is golden brown and crunchy, looking almost like clusters of granola, 15–20 minutes. Let cool before munching or topping.

tangy chocolate frosting

*Makes about 4 cups/865g/
enough for 1 large sheet cake,
2 smaller sheet cakes,
or one 9-inch layer cake*

2 sticks/8 ounces/225g unsalted butter, at room temperature

1½ cups/180g powdered sugar

Kosher salt

12 ounces/340g bittersweet chocolate, chopped

1 cup/220g full-fat sour cream, at room temperature

Use for
Cakes, any time you want or need chocolate frosting.

Do ahead
The frosting is really best used right after it's made for optimal spreadability, but it can be made 1 week ahead and kept refrigerated. Bring to room temperature and give it another spin in the mixer to properly soften before using.

This frosting is a contradiction. It's light but decadent, tangy, and bittersweet. Spreadable, silky and smooth, with none of the usual alchemy involved with a buttercream. It comes together effortlessly and tastes the same every single time. It's a miracle, really, irresistible even to those who claim not to love chocolate (me).

1   In a stand mixer fitted with the paddle (or in a bowl with an electric hand mixer), beat together the butter, powdered sugar, and a good pinch of salt on medium-high speed until light, fluffy, and very spreadable.

2   Microwave the chocolate in 20- or 30-second bursts until melted. (Or do this in a metal bowl over a small pot of simmering water.) Let cool for a few minutes. Using a spatula, stir the sour cream into the melted chocolate (it will thicken up considerably, almost turn paste-like—this is okay).

3   Add the chocolate mixture to the butter mixture and beat, scraping down the sides occasionally, until all is incorporated and the mixture looks smooth, fluffy, and spreadable, 3–4 minutes. Give it a taste and season with more salt, if needed.

salty vanilla frosting

Makes about 4 cups/865g/ enough for 1 large sheet cake, 2 smaller sheet cakes, or one 9-inch layer cake

2 sticks/8 ounces/225g unsalted butter, at room temperature

2 (8-ounce/225g) packages cream cheese, at room temperature

2½ cups/300g powdered sugar

½ teaspoon/2g kosher salt, plus more to taste

Vanilla bean, halved lengthwise, or 1 teaspoon vanilla extract

Use for
Either of the sheet cakes (page 108 or page 112), the Banana Split Ice Cream Cake (page 194), the Mint and Chip Ice Cream Cake (204; in lieu of the whipped cream), Brown Butter Pumpkin Cake (page 122), or Cold Carrot Cake (page 101).

Do ahead
The frosting is really best used right after it's made for optimal spreadability, but it can be made 1 week ahead and kept refrigerated. Bring to room temperature and give it another spin in the mixer to properly soften before using.

This is a sort of hybrid basic-buttercream/cream cheese frosting, combining the best of both worlds. It's salty, it's rich, it goes with everything, and if I'm forced to choose between this and chocolate, it's this every time. No questions asked. Great for any cake in this book, even the ice cream cakes—the texture is perfection even when frozen. What more could you ask for?

1   In a stand mixer fitted with the paddle (or in a bowl using an electric hand mixer), beat the butter on medium-high speed until light, fluffy, and very spreadable, 5–7 minutes.

2   Add the cream cheese, a little knob at a time, and continue to beat until well blended, another 2–3 minutes.

3   Add the powdered sugar and beat until combined. Add the salt and scrape in the vanilla seeds (or add the extract) and continue to beat, scraping down the sides occasionally, until extremely smooth, fluffy, and spreadable, 3–4 minutes. Give it a taste and season with more salt, if needed.

thank you

To Chris Bernabeo, thank you for taking a chance on doing something new. Your eye is brilliant, taste in music impeccable, work ethic and spirit unwavering. I could quite literally not have made this book without you. It was such a gift to make something for the first time together. Your talent knows no bounds and I can't wait to watch you become my most famous friend. Taylor—call him!

Britt Cobb, you brilliant genius who took the contents of a mood board and some word salad and turned them into the book design of my dreams. Thank you for making something equal parts interesting, familiar, new, iconic, beautiful, and above all: useful. A true honor to collaborate with you.

To Jane Morgan, for your schlepping and prepping, measuring and re-measuring, for feeding us beautiful food on set, for going to the store one million times and never forgetting the Cheez-Its. To Tori Schoen, for helping push the manuscript through, keeping me on track and my calendar/inbox uncluttered through the worst of it. To all the recipe testers: Gaby, Tom, Lauren, Sam, Jane, and Fatima. Thank you for your time, palates, and honesty to make sure these recipes work (and taste wonderful).

To the North Fork, Bloomville, and Brooklyn for your produce, sunshine on demand, and overcast days when we needed them. A special thank-you to Sarah-Sophie Flick, Jesse Peretz, and your whole family for allowing us into your home, and Scott DeSimon for lending us your pond, boat, and cool Italian towel.

To my gorgeous friends who are actually all models: Aminatou, Coco, Dusty, Shannon, Ebon, The Two Guys at Coney Island, The Woman in the Poodle Sweatshirt, Lauren, Patch, Lilli, Susan, Danny, Scott, Maya, Chelsea, Alexandra and Baby James, Syd, Clayton and Rodman and Amiel. Not modeling is hard! To Dora Fung for pulling the most glorious, fun outfits for us to play dress-up in.

To my editor, Francis Lam: Everyone knows you're the best, and now I know it too. Thanks for getting me, seeing me, and making me smarter by proxy. I'm sorry this manuscript was so late, really.

To my copyeditor, Kate Slate: you made me laugh with your matter-of-fact queries and zero tolerance for nonsense. I dedicate the peaches and cream recipe to you (if you can find it).

To Darian Keels, Stephanie Huntwork, Mark McCauslin, Kim Tyner, Allison Renzulli, Joey Lozada, Jana Branson, Kate Tyler, and the whole Clarkson Potter team: I'm so grateful for your support, advocacy, and unbridled enthusiasm for each book baby.

To Glynnis Albright, for being so gracious.

To my book agent, Nicole Tourtelot, for always going to bat for me and humoring my every meltdown for the third book in a row. My lowest number of meltdowns yet, I think!

To Dan and the rest of our Home Movies family. I can't wait to teach Dan how to make all these desserts on camera.

To David, "for everything," thanks for sharing a brain.

To Molly, for always seeing me and working toward "the big picture."

To Ron Mendoza and William Werner, for your mentorship, patience, guidance, and tutelage. Everything I know, I learned from you (except the bad habits, those are mine). Thank you for showing me desserts didn't have to be too sweet, that pastry cooks cooked too, that everything needs salt, and that fruit is a miracle.

To Christina Tosi, for teaching me that "good" is not good enough until it's "really fucking good." To Sarah Senneh, for teaching me how to make flawless biscuits and pie crust (and have the most fun while doing it). To Karen, for not telling Ron to fire me (sorry for the early grays), and to Yewande, for also loving raw pie dough. To everyone I ever shared a pastry kitchen with, thank you for inspiring and pushing me, laughing, singing, crying, and cleaning with me.

To Claudia Fleming, Lindsey Shere, Dorie Greenspan, and Michel Bras, for authoring my favorite books on dessert, the ones I pored over and learned from before I ever made my first galette.

To everyone else in my life who helps me keep the wheels on, my partners in life: I love you more than you know. I'm sorry I don't have the page count to name you all but IYKYK.

To everyone who stuck around, who kept reading, cooking and baking, liking and subscribing: Thank you for giving me someone to write for and a reason to cook. I love you, I love you, I love you.

index

Q

R

S

Clarkson Potter / Publishers
New York
clarksonpotter.com

Cover design: Britt Cobb
Cover photographs: Chris Bernabeo